How the Church Can Help WHERE DELINQUENCY BEGINS

How the Church can help

where

DELINQUENCY

begins

by Guy L. Roberts

John Knox Press
RICHMOND, VIRGINIA

Library of Congress Catalog Card Number: 58-7770

To all problem children who have not found adequate help in the solution of their problems—to the confused and distressed, to those who would "like to go straight but keep messing up and don't know why," this book is dedicated.

Preface

In view of the fact that so much has been written about juvenile delinquency—far too much, this writer thinks—why should another book be written? And, feeling this way, why would I write it? Well, there are two reasons: (1) I have come to feel strongly, after several years of extensive work with our problem children and their families, that the Church has a vital role, perhaps the key role, to play in both the prevention and cure of their mental and social ills. Furthermore, while a growing number of religious leaders are recognizing this fact, the general public and the vast majority of church members do not yet see the Church, or their churches, in this light. (2) Other students of this general problem, having become acquainted with my research and certain findings, suggested that these should be more widely published. With reluctance this book was begun.

The core material has been taken from a study, *The Religious Backgrounds and Attitudes of One Hundred Fifty Protestant Juvenile Delinquents,* made at the University of Pittsburgh in 1952. But as the book grew, it moved far afield, drawing material and insights from a much wider range. The focal point of writing is upon the delinquent and near delinquent. But always in the margin of thought is the neurotic youngster who may become a more serious problem than the delinquent and whose illness stems from a very similar background. Its configuration of causative factors is different, but the basic elements overlap widely. Hence the many references to both the delinquent and the neurotic, to both the socially ill and the mentally ill. The same program that may be developed by the churches for the prevention of the one can be applied with little change and almost equal effectiveness to the other. The problem child may be either delinquent or neurotic—or both.

The book is addressed to ministers and to lay officials of our churches—to church school teachers, to youth counselors, and to men's and women's groups—that they may move forward more rapidly toward the full realization of the potentialities of the Church in the actualities of prevention and cure. It is also addressed to public school teachers, social workers, and staff members of the many agencies that serve well in this field, that they may recognize more clearly the Church's role and co-operate more fully with the churches of their locale in joint community action. Finally, it is addressed to parents and neighbors of children who are clearly troubled and are showing symptoms of delinquent or neurotic behavior, that they too may see more clearly how their churches can help them with their problems and that they may utilize their churches more fully in their family lives. Thus there is a broad mixture of technical and statistical information and general information, attitudes, and opinions.

The "You" and "Your," as frequently used, refer not only to these parents but to all of "you" who are interested in and who work with children and youth. In a very real sense they are your children and the Church's children, for they are the children of the community and of God. They will influence your life and you will influence theirs—for good or ill. And the Church is your Church, whether or not you are a listed member of one of its fellowships. It is the institutional Body through which the eternal Christ is still working for the redemption of man—to seek and to save the least and the lost; to serve the bewildered, the confused, the problem child. Ought not we use it more fully? As never before in history it is awakening to its responsibility and opportunity in this area of life and is preparing to serve as it ought.

Part of chapter 2 appeared as an article in *The Christian Home,*

July, 1953. My gratitude is hereby expressed to the publishers for permission to use it here. I also wish to thank the many publishers of the books from which quotations are taken. And I especially am indebted to Elaine Holcomb for the encouragement she has given and the material she has provided from her very recent research in the field of delinquency. Mostly I am endebted to the many problem children with whom I have talked and who poured out their problems, their bewilderment, and their hopes and disappointments, in the counseling process.

GUY L. ROBERTS.

Contents

		PAGE
1.	Five Delinquent Children	15
2.	Is Your Child a Potential Delinquent?	31
3.	The Church Is Concerned	45
4.	The Problem Child Is Religious	61
5.	The Church and Our Homes	75
6.	The Redeeming Fellowship	97
7.	The Pastor as Counselor	117
8.	The Church and Its Allies	135
	Notes and Acknowledgments	155

How the Church Can Help WHERE DELINQUENCY BEGINS

1.

Five Delinquent Children

GEORGE WAS A SMALL WHITE BOY, 18 years old, immature and dull in appearance. He was co-operative and answered questions freely but had little to say except when questioned. George was the youngest of three brothers; his father and mother were divorced when he was eight years old. He didn't remember much that occurred before the divorce, except that his father got drunk often and beat his mother. His general manner at this point in the interview indicated at least a partial repression of unhappy childhood experiences.

After the separation of his parents George lived with his grandmother and aunt for a little more than a year, was then in an orphanage for two years, returned to his aunt for a while, and finally went to live with his mother, who had remarried. He was glad to be back with his mother and brothers but was soon getting into trouble. He didn't like school, wouldn't study, and failed in several of his subjects. He would "play hooky," stay out late at night, and was in trouble frequently at home and with the neighbors. George was not specific, in fact he was rather evasive, regarding the nature of his trouble with the neighbors. His mother tried to punish him but was too ill most of the time; she has since died. The stepfather punished him a few times, but George's father threatened to have him sued if he continued to beat the boy. Then the oldest brother was given the job of punishing George for his misdemeanors.

Information from other members of the family revealed that George's mother was badly mistreated by his father. She was frequently beaten so severely that the neighbors interfered and called the police. Several times she was locked in the cellar all day. After the divorce and remarriage of his mother, George was encouraged by his father to annoy and disobey his mother. He would throw garbage on the neighbor's porch and sometimes urinate or even defecate there. He was referred to as a regular Dr. Jekyll and Mr. Hyde—"as nice as he could be at times and then would act like the very devil." The family finally gave up hope of controlling him and had him committed to a training school, charged with truancy and incorrigibility.

After two years George was released to his mother and stepfather, but his behavior was no better. He would stay out until "all hours of the night" and was completely indifferent to the wishes or demands of the family. Being 16 years of age, he was given a work permit and a job was found for him in a printer's shop. He was also permitted to room with another working boy in the home of his aunt. While there he stole some money from his roommate and his aunt. He was suspected, apprehended, and committed to the institution where the writer met him.

Institutional records showed that he ran away several times; he was characterized as being dull, passive, immature, amoral, a victim of other boys in homosexual activities, poor in school work but fair at his occupation of baker's helper. His I.Q. was reported as being considerably below average. The Rorschach emphasized immaturity, anxiety, fear of authoritative figures, inability to handle emotional situations, difficulty in concentrating, unevenness in performance, superficiality in thinking, lack of intellectual drive, passivity, and a psychopathic personality.

George's test scores and conversation revealed no apparent religious interest or activity on the part of his father. His mother attended church and read the Bible occasionally and seemed to be very much interested in religion. He seldom attended Sunday school during early childhood, though he liked it "a little." No other church activities were attended that he could remember. During late childhood he attended Sunday school occasionally, "had nothing against it," but seldom prayed and never attended youth meetings or other church activities. The test showed his religious feelings to be largely neutral. Most of the items were checked "seldom" or "never," with the exception of "often having feelings of wanting to help people." He did not join a church and discontinued Sunday school at about age 13.

His test scores showed an attitude neutral toward the Church and mildly positive toward the Bible and God's influence in life. Some inconsistency was shown in these sections of the test but no more than could be expected from the type of personality the Rorschach showed George to be. In fact, his test scores on the whole seemed quite realistic. He stated that he had nothing against the Church but "it hasn't helped me." His attitude was quite definitely neutral. Furthermore, he "read the Bible through while in jail [in confinement at the institution]. There was nothing else to do. I didn't understand much of it but think it is O.K." And he reported a belief in God part of the time but with occasional doubts, saying "you can't prove it." His self-rating in Christian living was low. He believed that his mother was sincerely religious but rated the religious quality of the home as a little below average. George believed his answers were honestly given. "There was no point in lying," he said.

This is the case of a boy in whose early childhood deep anxiety and repressed rage became established; then, later, he became the victim of a vengeful father's spite against his former wife. Mental confusion, stifled personality development, and perverse outbursts of behavior were inevitable. He needed a foster home and the professional service of a child guidance clinic.

BOB WAS A GOOD-LOOKING NEGRO BOY, 18 years of age, above average in height, and well-built but not heavy. He was somewhat surly and noncommunicative at first but eased up and talked freely during the latter part of the interview. He was "always getting into trouble at school" and frequently fought with "the neighbor kids." Most of the neighbors would not let their children play with him; this made the problem worse. "No one could whip me there," he said, grinning, "nor here" (the school for delinquents to which he had been committed). He got along all right with his mother, but his father often beat him, "until I was too big." He admitted that a lot of it was his fault and that he had "a chip on my shoulder."

His father had a good job, and home conditions were economically satisfactory. Both parents were members of a Baptist church and active in church affairs. There was little worship in the home— grace at mealtime, periodically; prayers at bedtime when he was small, with an occasional Bible story read by his mother; sometimes his father read the Bible, though not often. His father and mother quarreled a lot, and the father was once jailed for beating the mother. It was evident from the discussion at this point that his father was very harsh, even brutal, in his methods of discipline.

Bob was compelled to attend Sunday school regularly during childhood but didn't particularly like it or dislike it. He skipped going frequently during later childhood and discontinued altogether at about the age of 14. His church attendance was only occasional during childhood and seldom or never during the teen years. He never attended Junior League or Youth Fellowship activities, not getting along well with "the kids," and was sometimes beaten for skipping Sunday school.

His religious feelings and attitudes were largely neutral or mixed, with positive attitudes slightly predominant. As he recalled his early training in Sunday school and home, he liked it, especially the Bible stories. Sometimes he believed in God but often doubted. He thought that church was good for most people and that prayer helped some people, but he could get along without them. He rated his home as partly Christian but himself as not Christian at all. His parents, he felt, didn't show enough Christianity at home. During his boyhood he had often prayed that there would be less trouble at home, and that he would not get into trouble at school or be sent away, "but it didn't help." So he gave up the prayer habit. Further conversation revealed a more or less impersonal attitude toward the Church and religion in general. He was intelligent enough to recognize the inconsistency displayed by his parents, particularly his father, and that religion has value for most people; but he had decided to ignore it.

Conflict between Bob and his father, and his aggressiveness with "other kids," grew worse during the early teens. He broke windows in a neighbor's home and ran away to avoid another beating. After three days of hiding out, sleeping wherever he could find a place, and stealing food, he was picked up by the police and taken to the juvenile court detention home. At the hearing he was placed on probation and returned to his home. With part-time work, more spending money, and being temporarily free of school (and neighborhood) irritations, he got through the summer all right, enduring his father's harsh supervision and distrust. Later in the fall he was accused of sexual improprieties with a girl and, on top of that, of sending an obscene letter to a woman teacher. The latter he stoutly denied, claiming that he was falsely accused by "other kids to get even with me." He admitted in part the sexual impropriety but claimed that it was exaggerated and that he did no more than the "other kids were doing or she welcomed." But because he was on probation he felt that he "had to take the rap." He was very bitter.

His institutional behavior was satisfactory on the surface. (He had been at the school 21 months.) But it was rated as "institutional adjustment," meeting the minimum requirements to avoid trouble with officers. For the most part he was rather seclusive, often quarrelsome, and had few friends.

He had two older brothers—one in the Navy—and a sister who was a student nurse. The brothers also had some trouble with their dad but not as much as he. His I.Q. was 110, and the Rorschach Test showed uneven reactions, indications of much aggressiveness, some anxiety, particularly with sex symbols, and poor contact with people but fair contact with his environment.

This is the case of a boy who apparently had a severe inner emotional conflict that brought him into a steadily increasing conflict with his father and neighbors. His progressive social deterioration

and religious negativism or neutralism and destructive aggressiveness can be largely traced to the cruelty of his father, who was outwardly religious (probably sincerely so) but lacked a truly Christian
spirit. He could not be broken but became a rebel and anti-social
—a boy with a chip on his shoulder. Having a high-normal intelligence, he could dissociate the Church, Bible, and religion in general
from apparent shortcomings in his own home and judge them to be
of some value. Yet he was so absorbed in his own emotional conflict
and his defenses were so strongly built that religion failed to function
as a dynamic force in his life.

BELLE WAS A LIGHT-COMPLEXIONED NEGRO GIRL,
tall and well-built, 17.5 years of age, and was quite friendly and
co-operative. She had only the vaguest memory of her mother
and no memory of her father, who deserted the family shortly
after she was born. She was in a "foundling home" for about
a year, returned to her mother for a time, was neglected and under-
nourished, and was adopted by her mother's cousin and his wife
shortly before she was three. She was the only child in the home of
her foster parents, who brought her north with them to the city
where she had spent most of her life.

Her foster parents, too, were Baptists, and quite active in their
church, although the foster mother (they will now be referred to as
her father and mother) was frequently ill and had to miss church.
Belle just took church life for granted and attended church, Sunday
school, and other church affairs regularly through early childhood.
She could remember nothing of her life before adoption but showed
evidences of repressed disturbances, and she was quite nervous. Her
early childhood with her present parents was uneventful so far as
she could recall and was not particularly happy or unhappy. She was
taught to pray at home and kept the habit. Her father sang in the
choir and was a deacon in his church. He read the Bible frequently
at home and occasionally read stories to her. She attended revival
meetings and was "converted," received instruction preparatory
to church membership and joined the church at about the age of
fifteen.

Belle's recent religious feelings were reported as being positive in most instances, with some feelings of alienation from God, not being forgiven, and struggles with her conscience. Her religious attitudes were, on the whole, strongly positive, her belief in the existence of God unquestioning, and she thought of herself as being "about average" in Christian living. She believed that she had tried hard to be a good Christian but had "too much trouble with mother." Her Biblical knowledge was considerably above the average of the group tested and she had received several Sunday school awards as proof of regular attendance. She stated that the church "helped people to be born again," and that "if young people took it more seriously they wouldn't go astray." "Jesus," she stated, "is the maker of all things, and we need Him in all that we do." And she believed very much in prayer, observing that "when you pray right you feel like you have been reconverted.",

There was much conflict between Belle and her mother during early adolescence. The mother, according to the case worker's report, was a hypochondriac and chronic complainer, frequently beating and constantly scolding and accusing the girl. Jealousy was the attributed motive. The father tried to be nice to Belle, and she, of course, was openly partial to him. If he tried to defend her it brought him into conflict with the mother; so he finally pursued a more or less neutral course, interfering as little as possible. Conflict became so intense that Belle, too, ran away but was soon apprehended, taken to juvenile court, and committed to a school for delinquent girls.

After a year she was released to her parents, but the old conflict continued and she was recommitted about ten months later. Belle insisted that she did not frequent "bad places" nor run around in a "bad group" as she was accused of doing. She frankly reported that she had taken a few social drinks and had intercourse two or three times with one boy whom she was "in love with" and still expected or hoped to marry. She didn't think that was very wrong, saying, "the Bible says nothing against it." With apparent honesty she denied being promiscuous as accused by her mother. But at the court hearing she admitted to more than she had done so the judge would send her away. She preferred to live at the institution rather than with her mother.

Her conduct at the institution was varied, though mostly satisfactory. She was usually obedient and co-operative but given to occasional moody spells, at which times she was disobedient or impudent and showed temper displays. Sometimes she was ridiculed by other girls when she "talked religion" to them. Both her pastor and the institutional chaplain thought of her as being sincerely religious, and the former agreed that her parents were active in the program of their church. She was apparently quite frank and honest in her interview conversation and in her test replies.

Her I.Q. was 92. The Rorschach revealed considerable anxiety, emotional immaturity and superficiality in thinking, some tenseness and insecurity, and poor identification with people but fair contact with environment.

This is the case of a neglected and unwanted child whose early childhood insecurity was further aggravated by a jealous and nagging, deeply neurotic foster mother—hence the hunger for love and the disobedience that got her into trouble. She was sincerely religious and orthodox in her thinking, but she could find no resolution of the conflict situation.

IRVIN WAS A QUIET AND APPARENTLY INTROVERTED WHITE BOY, 17 years of age, tall and slender. His attitude was not at all antagonistic or suspicious during interviews, but he was somewhat withdrawn, aloof, living largely within himself and giving out to the world no more than was asked, though he later became more friendly and co-operative.

He reported his father as being a United Brethren and his mother a Methodist. Both attended church occasionally to regularly, though the father was not a member. They seemed to believe strongly in their religion and liked their church. But neither of them held any office or position of responsibility in the church so far as he knew. Grace was said at mealtime, but there was no other family worship in the home. He was taught to say his prayers, and continued to do

so all during childhood. Sometimes his mother was seen to be reading the Bible—but seldom, and the father never that he could recall.
He attended Sunday school regularly in childhood and occasionally
in early adolescence. He never attended youth group activities—
his church being small had no organized youth group—and rarely
attended church service. He stopped saying prayers at about the age
of twelve and seldom went to Sunday school after he was fourteen.
He was baptized in infancy but did not later join the church.

Irvin's recent religious feelings were reported as being largely
neutral, with some confused feelings and an occasional wish to be
helpful. His attitudes toward the Church and the Bible were positive,
though not as strongly so as some others. While he believed in the
existence of God, with occasional doubts, he had no awareness of
God's influence in his life. He rated his home as average in its
Christian influence and his own character as about average. He explained his attitude toward God as in no manner implying antago-
nism or opposition to the idea of God's helping other people, but
he had no sense of God within his own life. Sometimes he doubted
the existence of God when he saw so many wrong things in life
and people getting away with so much. Concerning his own self-
rating, he stated that he was thinking of himself merely as a person
rather than in the particular sense of being a Christian. He felt that
his answers throughout the test expressed his opinions quite well.
(The test was discussed during a personal interview.) He stated that
he had no opposition to the church and believed that it did a lot
of good and that it might have helped him more if he had been
more deeply interested and had taken a more active part.

Irvin was the youngest of five children. His father was killed
when he was two years old. His mother remarried. Thus his
references to his father on the test related to his stepfather, who was
the only father he really knew. He "got along okay at home but not
so well at school." Not liking to study, he was often truant—"couldn't
keep my mind on my work." Truancy was a factor, though secondary, in his delinquency. Irvin got "into trouble with some other boys"
(stealing) and was placed on probation. He spent the summer at a

camp where his uncle worked, "to try to stay out of trouble." But the following winter he was with some boys who broke into a store and took some things. He was committed to a school for delinquents. He didn't know why he did it—he "just went along." His father was a laborer and had steady work, but with a large family, money was scarce and they lived in a socially unfavorable neighborhood. Poverty was not a primary factor.

His I.Q. was 108 and his personality characterized as showing strong tendencies toward fantasy, being easily influenced and immature, and suffering from repressed anxiety. There was also poor relationship to other people and limited capacity for emotional living.

Here apparently is the case of a boy whose very early childhood was somewhat deficient in true affection and the death of whose father caused at least a slight trauma. While there was no evidence of serious conflict or open hostility in the home, there was evidently a lack of positive training, discipline, and true warmth of affection, at least in a form of expression that he could receive. He grew up ruled largely by his own whims and fantasies, living behind his inner defenses most of the time but occasionally coming out to be influenced by whoever offered something interesting at the moment. His discipline was left largely in the hands of his mother, who had probably grown tired of her family responsibilities. Thus he alternated between seclusiveness and a "follow the leader" dependency. Religion was accepted ideationally, but as a dynamic force it never penetrated his inner defenses.

FAY WAS A 17-YEAR-OLD WHITE GIRL OF ABOUT MEDIUM HEIGHT, a little coarse of feature but neither homely nor especially attractive. She was friendly, co-operative, and easy in conversation.

Both parents came to this country from central Europe, where the father had been reared Catholic and the mother Lutheran. They lived in a mill town adjacent to a large city. There apparently were no serious family problems, economically or otherwise, until the father's death when Fay was about eleven—or during the preceding year in which he was seriously ill most of the time. She was the youngest of six children, with three older sisters and two brothers. The mother did not remarry but tried to support the family herself, with the help of the older children who one by one found part-time or full-time work. But the father's long illness had brought indebtedness, and family earnings were insufficient for several years. During this time they were on and off public assistance and compelled to live in a poor neighborhood.

After coming to this country the father attended no church except for special occasions but "believed in religion." The mother and children attended occasionally (fairly often, Fay thought) a small Lutheran church. Later the mother joined a small religious sect, when Fay was about seven or eight years of age. She went with her mother to their meetings a few times but didn't like them and continued to attend the Lutheran Sunday school more or less regularly, the church service occasionally, but took part in no other church activity. The church being small had no Junior League or youth fellowship program.

"Things were all right until father died," said Fay. "Then everything seemed to go wrong." The mother could not handle the children. "She fussed at us a lot and was always wrangling about money and where we went." Religion, too, was a source of family friction. Her mother read the Bible regularly and irritated the children with her arguments. They, at least Fay, thought her a fanatic. The older sisters got work and helped ease the financial strain, but the boys "didn't pay much attention" to their mother, going out when and where they pleased. Fay, now thirteen, began staying out late after school—partly to avoid the unpleasant home situation and partly in imitation of her brothers, envying them their freedom. The older sisters "sometimes sided with me and sometimes with mother." Later, however, as Fay became more resistant to supervision, the girls supported their mother in most of the conflicts.

However, the more the family opposed her the more rebellious she became. She would stay out late at night and was often truant. Also she began "running around" with a girl and dating boys, which action was strongly opposed by the family. She persisted, however, and stayed out all night one time, the two couples sleeping in the car. Her mother had been accusing her of promiscuity. This she denied, but admitted having sexual intercourse with the one boy. She was taken to juvenile court, charged with sex delinquency and incorrigibility and sent to a school for young, first-offending delinquent girls. She was not quite fifteen. Because of her intelligence and the good early impressions she made, she was given special privileges and was permitted to work in a private home and attend a public high school. But in school she stole some items from another pupil's locker and was committed to the institution where interviewed by the writer. Her behavior there was quite satisfactory.

Fay's I.Q. was well above average, with a Bellevue Wechsler rating of 112 (f.s.) and an Otis rating of 124. The Rorschach also revealed high-average intelligence, wide range of interests but lack of intellectual drive, some immaturity, some anxiety, but good environmental contact, and capability of socially acceptable behavior.

She received instruction in the Catechism and joined the church at the age of 14, but discontinued attendance at Sunday school. Her test scores revealed generally positive religious feelings with some confused feelings and with a sense of alienation from God. Attitudes toward the Church, Bible, and God were consistently positive. Her Biblical knowledge score was high. She reported a strong belief in God, rated herself as being "about average" in Christian living and her home as average in Christian character. "Jesus," she said, "is the most wonderful person who ever lived," and prayer helps by "bringing you nearer to God." (She said her prayers occasionally at bedtime.) She found no fault with her church, but "it didn't help me much, because I didn't go regularly." Her home religious training could have been improved, she thought, "for when mother tried to talk about religion, I used to think she was preaching and it annoyed me." Again she said, "I believe in God and the Church, and I try to be a Christian, but things just went wrong and I don't know why."

This is the case of a youngest child in a fairly large family whose mother was a "nervous," at least mildly neurotic, person who had grown tired of her responsibilities even before her husband's death and who had never conveyed an adequate love to the child. Then came the death of the father, to whom Fay was strongly attached, right at the critical age when this attachment means most to a girl. Denied love and a nice home and the things an intelligent and sensitive girl desires, she blindly sought whatever substitute satisfactions her neighborhood afforded. This resulted in an ever-growing conflict with her conscientious but inadequate mother and the final behavior characterized as delinquency.

THESE FIVE YOUNG PEOPLE WERE KNOWN WELL BY THE WRITER. Their stories are not told as if typical of all delinquents. No five cases could be typical. But they are fairly representative of the Protestant delinquent population of a large eastern state. They illustrate the two truths that I wish to present at this point; namely, that the Church has had its chance with most of these problem children but has failed them, *and that their attitudes toward the Church and religion are such that the Church still has the opportunity of playing a vital role in their social rehabilitation.* The large majority of them are basically religious, but frustrated and confused. Recall Fay's statement above about believing and wanting to be a Christian but things kept going wrong and she didn't know why. It was typical of many. One of the boys expressed it this way: "I want to go straight. I want to be a Christian and I think I am, but I keep messing up and don't know why."

But these five young people were "branded" as being delinquent and were institutionalized—an accusation that they were unsafe, too tough to be left loose among us, or an admission that we in this modern age of enlightenment do not yet know how to help our children solve their deeper problems. Perhaps one of these five needed a short period of institutional care. Conflict at home, a prolonged frustration, a despair-born rebellion got them into trouble. It is most difficult to determine just how many like them are dragged through the courts for juvenile offenders, charged with delinquency, and committed to institutions or placed on probation. But the number runs into the hundreds of thousands in the United States.

Accurate statistics are not available in many places and what is termed "delinquency" varies from place to place.

They come from the big cities, the small industrial towns, and from rural areas. Mostly they come from the "slums," "delinquent areas," the socially and economically unfavorable neighborhoods. In the cities it is the downtown district and the areas bordering the business district or adjacent to rivers. But delinquent behavior is not limited to these. Youthful offenders of the more prosperous communities are better "taken care of" and fewer reach the courts —very few, the institutions. Problems are greater in these less favored areas, and the "kids" have less help in solving problems of adjustment. There is more pressure, tension, conflict, and frustration. There is less satisfaction of a child's basic needs, more temptation, more rebellion.

Fay's parents were foreign-born—she a second-generation American. There are more from similar homes than from an equal number of "American" homes—Americans of longer standing. Adjustments are more difficult for second-generation Americans. Their problems are more complex. Two of the five cases reported above are Negroes. That is roughly typical. The ratio varies from community to community, but the incidence of juvenile court cases among Negroes is perhaps three times that of their population ratio. In some localities it is much more than that. In the area studied by the writer, and the two institutions serving it, the Negro delinquent population was about 45 per cent, while the Negro population of the area was less than 25 per cent. This is no reflection upon the basic character of the Negro but an indictment against white prejudice and injustice. One hundred years of freedom from slavery should have brought them to a more nearly equal social-economic level. White prejudice and indifference—lack of an Amos-spirit of justice—is largely responsible for impeding the rise of the Negro.

And the big majority of our delinquent children are boys. Are boys worse than girls? Well, perhaps they are more aggressive, proportionately more extrovert, more rebellious. Perhaps our culture has conditioned our girls to greater conformity. Perhaps the female is more conservative by nature. Perhaps modern society retains a little of the old chivalry and is more considerate of its women and girls, slower to convict of crime or charge with delinquency. Anyway, for every girl committed, from three to five boys are committed to institutions for delinquent children.

Now let's take a look at your children.

2.

Is Your Child a Potential Delinquent?

YES, AND SO IS MINE. All children are potential delinquents, for all children have problems that may become too difficult for them to solve. The problem child is the child with an unescapable problem, which he cannot solve adequately. Circumstances could develop that would confront any child with a problem beyond his powers.

During the next twelve months scores of thousands of such children in the United States will be committed to institutions for delinquents. More than three hundred thousand additional boys and girls will become involved in misdemeanors similar in cause and seriousness but will not be committed to institutions because parents or social agencies will be able to make other arrangements. Your child or mine could be one of these. But he need not be if we face the problem sensibly and do what any interested parent can do to help him solve his basic problem.

Juvenile delinquents are perhaps the most studied segment of our population and possibly the least understood. They have been investigated by government agencies. Innumerable national, state, and local conferences have been held to talk about them. Students, professors, social workers, and public officials have turned out thousands of books, pamphlets, and magazine articles on various aspects of their problem. Yet there is wide disagreement as to both the causative factors and the methods of treatment. Hirsch, noting this confusion of ideas and opinions, explained:

In spite of several excellent pieces of work in juvenile delinquency, much less is known of its causes, effective treatment
and prevention than is generally recognized or admitted. There
are a number of reasons for this state of inadequate knowledge,
one of which is inherent in the very nature of the subject matter.
Not only are the motivations of human beings notably of an
extreme complexity, but they are to a great extent submerged
in the unconscious. Furthermore, laboratory experiments are
in essence highly artificial if they deal with significant problems;
and when they particularize and concern themselves with such
problems as the special senses, they tend to be either stale or
irrelevant to criminology. Lastly, it is highly probable that the
intrinsic characteristics and motives of man are of such a nature
that they will not submit to measurement and, when we apply
mathematics and statistics to them, we merely compute and
correlate some of their effects and precipitates.[1]

Hirsch goes on to list heredity, environment, accident, and genius
as causal categories under which numerous specific factors are sub-
sumed. He challenges the significant position generally attributed
to the broken home and stresses the inherent deviations of parents
of the delinquent, finding both parents normal in only 20 per cent
of the cases studied. Citing the fact that 20 to 30 per cent produce
delinquents, he argues that the broken home itself is in large part
a result of the poor constitutional make-up of one or both parents.
"We assert that the poor milieu does not produce delinquency, but
may lead to it if the child has a constitution similar to the poor ones
of the parents."

The Gluecks, in their *Five Hundred Criminal Careers,* show that
84.8 per cent of the cases studied have criminal relatives, 24.8 per
cent criminal parents, 39.6 per cent a criminal sibling, and 18.8 per
cent had one or both parents and one or more siblings who were
criminal.[2] This would tend to bolster Hirsch's arguments; and
Sullenger writes, "Many studies of the family life of delinquent
children have revealed a high percentage of immoral backgrounds
and delinquency within the immediate family."[3] Healy, on the other
hand, is supported by Reckless and Smith in finding that most de-

linquents are normal young persons with unfortunate environments and that juvenile delinquency cannot be attributed to personality type, age, sex, race, nationality, or to biological factors—that it is the result of social factors such as the economic situation, size of family, broken homes, parent-child relations, social status, education and occupation, recreation facilities, neighborhood conditions, and school maladjustments; and that the juvenile delinquent is usually a normal child gone astray.[4]

These and many other studies of similar scope and findings indicate quite clearly that the causal factors are difficult to isolate and are poorly understood, the pattern no doubt varying from case to case. The findings of most students in the field appear to vary with their own particular bent or frame of reference, some finding congenital personality defects to be of primary importance while others find family relationships and community situations (sociological factors) to be the primary causes. Lindeman, while rejecting any inherited tendency toward crime, summarizes the matter by stating that the basic causes of crime are to be found in individual, psychological, mental and emotional defects on the one hand, and in the irregularities and malformations in our social institutions, legal practices, economic arrangements, and human relationships on the other hand.[5]

William Sheldon, in *Varieties of Delinquent Youth,* takes a different approach and presents a radically different answer as to both cause and cure of delinquency. He thinks of himself as a "constitutional psychologist" and works from the premise that behavior is a function of structure and that personality can best be interpreted and explained against the frame of reference of a taxonomic (medical classification) description of the physical constitution. From this viewpoint he studied the case records of 200 delinquent boys as related to body structure, using standardized medical photographs divided into somatotypes (body types). He found sufficient statistical association between delinquency and particular kinds of dysplasia (shape and structure variations) to convince himself that he was on the right track, that personality resides in the cells, and that delinquency is due to a lack of balance in the cell. He also found that the clue to delinquency is "abortive predation." The predatory attitude, in his judgment, is quite all right, even admirable, but the delinquent's failure is in his poor execution. Thus the victim gets caught, or he fails to discriminate between what society will permit or reject.[6]

Dr. Karl Menninger, in *Man Against Himself,* holding to the Freudian theory of the life instinct and death instinct and that both are either self-directed or directed toward others by early contacts and training, presents the interesting theory that much delinquency and crime are closely related to suicide in cause. This particularly relates to the compulsive type of delinquent behavior where the victim is perpetually being caught and punished. Due chiefly to inadequate, or inadequately expressed, love in his early childhood relationships, mainly within the family, the child grows up with resentment and aggressive feelings directed against his parents. These feelings are accompanied by guilt and cannot be expressed adequately against the parent. Thus they become partly expressed against other persons (society) and partly against self in the form of aggressive delinquent behavior that cannot help but bring punishment upon the offender. Thus, unconsciously, by punishing himself he is destroying his position in society. His character is akin to that of the alcoholic, neurotic invalid, and other forms of partial suicides.[7]

Dr. Menninger draws a clear distinction between the criminal who escapes punishment more often than not and whose criminal career is more or less a matter of free choice and those like the above whom he would designate as "neurotic criminals." Of such, he says: "having yielded to their aggressive impulses, [they] are obliged to surrender in the end to the threats of their own consciences if not to the intimidations of the law. This leads them, then, to seek punishment, to allow themselves to be caught, to commit provocative offenses or even to 'break into jail.' "[8] Thus Dr. Menninger presents the hypothesis that some anti-social behavior (delinquency) is a mask for self-destructive intentions, largely unconscious. Such a condition is found only where love was inadequately expressed in the home, even though to the casual observer and to the child himself, consciously, the conduct of the parents seemed above reproach. The fact that their conduct seemed above reproach to the child would increase his sense of guilt for the aggressive feelings toward them which he could not avoid having because he failed to receive adequate love. Not receiving love adequately, he could not love himself adequately, would blame himself and be driven compulsively into behavior patterns that would inevitably bring punishment upon both the offending parents and the guilty self. Such cases require psychotherapy.[9] But fortunately most delinquents are not motivated by such irresistible compulsions.

Looking back at the five young people in chapter 1, it is apparent that conflict in the family, between the child and a parent, was a characteristic situation, though not so pronounced in the case of Irvin. In his case there was more confusion and insecurity, resulting in more anxiety and less conscious and overt aggression. In the other four, aggression was more overt and direct, with somewhat less anxiety. But in all cases the anxiety-aggression axis prevailed. In addition to these two traits, the Rorschach tests revealed confused thinking, emotional immaturity, and poor contact with people as common characteristics. But these are symptoms of delinquency, not causes. The children were not innately that way.

The simple fact is that the delinquent child has a problem which he cannot escape or solve adequately. He is in a position similar to that of an eighth-grade boy suddenly placed in an advanced algebra class. The problems are too difficult—too many unknown factors and the formulas too complicated. Like that of a good teacher, our task is to help our bewildered youngster pick out the factors in his problem and find the formula by which he can solve it. Physical defects, mental deficiency, defective emotional responses, feelings of anxiety and insecurity, conflict or lack of affection in the home, moral turpitude on the part of other members of the family, poverty, social rejection, school difficulties, and numerous community situations are among the factors to look for. The pattern differs in every individual case. But in all cases love is inadequately expressed. *A primary function of the Church is to make love applicable in individual and family life. It should be our first source of help.*

Let us take a quick look at the problem of Earl, who was 15 years of age, medium in height, and slight of build when I last talked with him. His family were respectable, middle-class, old-stock Americans, and church people. His father, a salesman, was killed in an accident when Earl was four. This was a severe emotional shock to both the boy and his mother, but Earl appeared to take it in stride.

He and his mother made their home with her parents and an unmarried sister who taught school. His mother had been a music teacher and continued to teach a few private pupils. She mingled socially and was quite active in church work but never remarried. And she developed a mild case of self-pity—not bad, but noticeable.

Earl had accepted his grandfather as a father and was very fond of him. Then the grandfather died. Earl was seven. He never quite recovered from the double blow. Left to be reared by three women—mother, grandmother, and maiden aunt—he was smothered with femininity and protection. Earl was the "Little Lord Fauntleroy" of his neighborhood. He dressed better than the neighbor children, had to study his music and be the "nice boy" his "poor dear mamma" wanted him to be, not to mention "auntie" and "grams." Football on the vacant lot, hikes in the woods, and swimming in the creek by the railroad trestle were prohibited. Held in disdain by the neighborhood boys, victim of their gibes, he developed deep resentments and a sense of inferiority. His mother loved him, but her love was inadequately expressed.

At the age of 13 Earl rifled a teacher's desk, stole a few things and damaged more. That Earl would do such a thing was unbelievable to those who thought they knew him. For the sake of the family he got off with light punishment, but he was watched over by his family even more closely and constantly reminded to "be a good boy and don't disgrace mamma." A few months later, with a younger boy, he broke into a small store, took a few items—nothing that he particularly wanted—and scattered other things all over the place. For this he was taken to juvenile court but was released on probation. The protective but suppressive home influence continued unabated and so did Earl's inner conflict. Five months later, and again with a younger companion, he knocked the glass out of the door of a house, opened the door, entered, and, apparently in a state of panic, literally tore the place apart. He was committed to a school for delinquents.

Earl's problem was that of a boy whose emotional responses were left slightly defective by the double shock of his father's and grandfather's deaths. And the women of the household did not permit him to attain ego maturity, self-reliance, and social acceptance by the neighborhood boys. His drive toward these goals was constantly blocked; and he sensed, consciously or unconsciously, that his mother was largely to blame. Toward her his resentment was directed, though not wholly consciously. Thus his suppressed resentment would break out periodically in a misdemeanor—partly to impress a younger and weaker boy (for recognition) and partly to punish his mother, whose frequent reminder to "be a good boy for mother's sake" was the chief blocking factor. Unable to solve his basic social problem acceptably, he erupted in an unacceptable manner. If Earl's mother and his minister had been alert to the help his church might have provided or made available, his break with society might well have been prevented.

A mother asked this question: "If delinquency is a social or environmental problem, why does only one child growing up in the same family and neighborhood with his brothers and sisters become a delinquent?" The answer is simply that six children in the same family do not have identical environments or problems. No two are identical in the physical, intellectual, or emotional endowments with which they meet their respective environments. And the mere fact that they are of different ages, attend different schools or classes, have different playmates, and occupy different positions in the family places them in different environments and confronts them with different problems. A review of Fay's story will illustrate this. (See chapter 1.)

Fay was the youngest of six children—three older sisters and two older brothers. Her father died when she was eleven—a critical point in her emotional relationship to him. Her older sisters had passed through this stage. Underlying the shock of death was the factor of serious quarreling between her parents that began at about the time of Fay's birth. Because of this domestic discord, and possibly other reasons, the mother failed to convey to Fay the warmth of love she needed in infancy, leaving her with a greater degree of insecurity than existed in the other children. For several months after the father's death anxiety over money matters was a disturbing factor. The mother was worried and nagged a lot. But the two older girls got work and relieved the financial problem. The family conflict slowly focused on Fay and her mother. They just couldn't hit it off. The older girls sided with Fay sometimes and with their mother sometimes. But as the situation worsened and Fay kept staying out later and later, all hands turned against her.

She had reached the age of 14, was intelligent, sensitive, insecure, and alienated from her family. Her drive was toward the security of affection and acceptance. Unable to solve the problem of finding it in the family, she turned to an older girl companion, with whom she double-dated, and to sexual intimacies with her boy friend in defiance of her family. She was charged with incorrigibility and sex delinquency and committed to a school for delinquent girls. There was no taint in her ancestry, no criminality in her immediate family, and no inherent mental defect. Her position in the family placed her in a situation greatly different from that of her siblings and posed a problem too difficult for her to solve. An alert church could have given her the security, acceptance, and affection she needed.

Of the 150 institutionalized delinquents investigated by the writer, 30 were carefully selected as most clearly representative of the larger group and studied more extensively. Of these 30, the broken home (by death, desertion, or divorce) was a factor in 23 cases. (This is much higher than the general average.) Serious family conflict involving the child occurred in 18 cases, while conflict of a lesser degree, yet serious enough to cause considerable pain and resentment, occurred in five other cases, and may have been a contributing factor in three others. The extent to which excessive drinking, more often by the father, and immoral conduct, particularly by the mother, were factors that contributed to the delinquency of their children could not be determined accurately. However, seven fathers were alleged to have drunk to excess and four mothers could be charged with immoral or morally unconventional behavior. Nine of the 30 were above average in intelligence, 13 were below, and 8 were average. The entire 150 cases averaged slightly below the general teen-age norm. And that minor difference can be accounted for on the basis of lack of interest and motivation to respond, or anxiety blocking, rather than any significant difference in innate intelligence. There is no one cause for a child's becoming delinquent in behavior. It is nearly always a constellation of factors, with each factor weighted differently in each case as to relative importance. Community and school conditions may provide contributing factors in the form of additional temptations, irritations, frustrations, etc., but the chief predisposing factor is a complex home situation where love is deficient or inadequately expressed, where there is conflict and confusion, extreme laxness or harshness in discipline, a feeling by the child of not being understood, loved, or wanted. Such home conditions may produce either delinquency or mental illness—the neurotic delinquent or the psycho-neurotic—or personalities that fluctuate between. The direction toward which the victim turns is determined partly by innate traits and partly by happenstance, incidental and accidental environment factors. In all such inadequate family situations the result is a problem child.

The role of "comic" books—picture stories of horror and amoral adventure—as a causative factor in delinquency has recently become a subject of popular discussion, especially by women's societies and parents' groups in churches. This interest has been greatly stimulated by *The Seduction of the Innocent,* a stimulating book by Frederic Wertham that vividly portrays the findings of the author, based on several years of research. The author gives an impressive array of evidence that convinces him and many of his readers that here is a primary cause that can be faced with specific action. But like many other environmental factors, the "comic" book may be, and often is, the precipitating, "kick-off," or "trigger" factor stimulating or structuring the immediate pattern of delinquent response. The percentage of children that read these horror and amoral adventure stories and are thus affected is relatively small. And in these cases of delinquent response, the more basic, predisposing factors were long since built into their personality structure by hereditary defects or, more commonly, by inadequate home life, inadequate love.

Deeply established attitudes and sentiments originating in childhood are the primary factors. It is these that determine the child's reaction to environmental factors and which largely determine his ability or inability to make a fair social adjustment regardless of any but the most serious hereditary defects. The attitudes and sentiments that predispose to delinquent or neurotic patterns of behavior are rooted in parental neglect and inadequate expression of love—in resentment, fear, and guilt; in fear of rejection, resentment because of it, and guilt for feeling the resentment; in fear that he is unworthy of love and unable to cope with life. Of much of this the child is unconscious. Sometimes these attitudes are caught from the parents' lack of faith, love, and emotional stability—a reflection of the parents' ego evolvement, defenses, inhibitions, or moral laxity. They may arise from a repressed or overtly expressed rebellion against these parental inadequacies. They sometimes arise in homes where the parents are good, well-intentioned, and personally and mentally well-adjusted persons who became frightened by the inadequate psychology of a generation ago and failed to discipline the child and to train for responsibility, fearing the exaggerated ill effects of suppression and frustration. Both restricted and required activity in a family atmosphere of understanding, faith, and love are beneficial and frequently necessary. Except in the few cases of serious genetic defects, faulty interpersonal relationships within the family is the primary and major cause of delinquent or neurotic behavior. *To re-create around the problem child a new pattern of wholesome interpersonal relationships based on understanding, faith, and love is the cure. This is a primary function of the Church.*

Extensive discussion of these more serious cases of delinquency has been given to point up more sharply the nature of the problem. But let us keep in mind that there are many true problem children for each one whose difficulties lead to committal in an institution. Their problems are similar in nature and often in degree. It is these, too, in whom we are interested, for they are the children in your home or your church. All these causative factors merely tend to produce delinquency but need not in most cases do so. They aggravate the problems that all children have, making them too difficult for the youngsters to solve alone. But given the help that the alert community and church could provide, few of our potential delinquents would become delinquent.

In the home, in the school, in the community, your child is striving for recognition, acceptance, affection, and the inner sense of security and worth that these provide. Without these he cannot love himself or others in a manner necessary for good social adjustment. If the family, school, or community offers too many difficulties—barriers that block this attainment—or if either heredity or early childhood conditioning has produced a defect or deficiency in the child's mechanism of adjustment, he may not be able to attain this necessary state of well-being without understanding help. The urgent need is unrelenting; the thwarting circumstances are ever present. He can't escape the problem; he can't solve it. Without an understanding guide or counselor (which is our job as parents) delinquency is almost inevitable. With such a parent or friend it would seldom occur. The degree of the child's deficiency and the extent of the thwarting circumstances will determine how much help he will need and whether or not it can be provided at home.

But how many parents do understand their teen-agers, especially at the beginning of that turbulent period? They are baffling to themselves and to everyone around them. The delinquent is just one of these same kids, only a little more so. All of them are potential delinquents but none of them need become so. The problems of youth are deep, deep problems. They all need counsel; some need more. Ah, but their powers of adjustment are almost limitless!

We parents need not know all the answers pertaining to our children and their problems. If that were necessary, we would all be in despair. These youngsters of ours are resilient and can take a lot of emotional or physical bumps. And they can survive a lot of our imperfections. But there are a few things we can easily learn, and learn to do, that will make it unlikely that our potential delinquents will become delinquent.

There is an old adage that has a lot of truth in it—allowing for oversimplification, of course: "Give them plenty of food and plenty of love and don't worry." Where the atmosphere of that adage prevails, the incidence of delinquency will be small. We may not be able to provide our kids with the luxuries our gadget-mad generation seems to crave, but we can provide them with adequate food. They don't need many of the luxury items. Only dire poverty is a serious factor in delinquency, and then it is accompanied by other conditions.

And we can give them love. If we are at all mature in our own emotional responses, we can keep our anxieties and our marital conflicts under moderate control so that love, confidence, and optimism are the prevailing moods.

Love means discipline—firmness as well as tenderness. Extreme laxness and apparent indifference to conduct make for insecurity, lack of confidence and self-control on the part of the child. "Thou shalt" and "thou shalt not" have a place in the family relationship. There ought to be a few definite "must's" and "must not's" clearly understood by the child, interpreted in so far as possible in terms of his understanding and experience, and enforced kindly but firmly. There are certain great moral imperatives that five thousand years of human history have proved to be valuable. These should be accepted by us parents and lived to the best of our ability, and no doubts should be left in the minds of our children regarding what we expect of them on these points.

But between these pillars of do's and don't's there are vast areas of conduct where relativity and change prevail. With justice and mercy, fairness, kindness, and good sportsmanship, as our guiding rule, problems in these fields should be worked out on an individual, give-and-take basis.

We can make our kids feel needed and wanted and important in our family organization by giving them specific responsibilities, working with them, and bringing them into the discussion of family problems. They should have an allowance in keeping with the realities of the economic situation, which they may spend as they please, subject to family consultation but not coercion (exceptions granted, of course). But they ought not to be paid for the various household chores they perform. That should be work of love, of family co-operation. It gives them a deeper sense of belonging.

We can do all this fairly well without reading a lot of psychology. "Psychology" is a good thing and works well on others. But it doesn't work so well on our own families. Love does, though, if it is mature and responsible. For love is both tender affection and resolute good will, both liberating and restraining. In homes where love is lived generously and wisely, delinquency is a rare occurrence. After three interviews and the establishment of full confidence, in a moment of deep insight an attractive, intelligent delinquent girl said to me, "All I've ever needed was the right kind of love."

Others have said, with slight variations but the same thought, "I want to go straight and I have tried to do right, but I keep messing up and don't know why." They do not know why. Our job as parents is to help them find out why, and help them before they "mess up" too much. A certain amount of social failure is inevitable. It is a part of the trial-and-error process of learning. But we parents need not permit our children to become too badly tangled emotionally and socially. If we can't help them solve their too-big problems, we can direct them to someone in the community or nearby city who can. This is our task. Our church is our best ally. It is the mediator of a divine love. It can provide the needed supplement where parental love is inadequate.

3.

The Church
Is Concerned

THE INTEREST OF THE CHURCH IN THE YOUTH of the community is readily admitted, but many will argue that this interest is a nebulous and impotent sentiment of little import as a deterrent to delinquency. How effectively has the Church expressed its concern? You have a right to ask. What is the Church at large doing to help problem families and children? And how can my church help in specific problem situations?

Many juvenile court judges, probation officers, and social workers have expressed opinions regarding the role of religion and the Church in the prevention of delinquency. Numerous studies have been made by departments of religion and psychology in universities and seminaries that touch upon the relationship of certain aspects of religion and church activity to delinquency or character development. Most of these studies have been confined to the measurement of certain types of information and activities, such as Biblical knowledge and Sunday school attendance, that come under the general category of character education. A few have attempted to measure attitudes. None, however, so far as the writer has been able to ascertain, has attempted to go deeply into the functioning of religion as a dynamic factor in the early life of the problem child. The findings of such studies have been quite inconclusive, and the expressed opinions of the above-mentioned professionals are varied and often confusing. They disagree as widely over this question as over the basic causes.

The report of a study conducted by staff members of the New

York State Department of Social Welfare points to the failure of the Church to reach delinquent children and states categorically that "The few children in the study who attended Sunday school or church were not deterred in their delinquency by such contacts."[1] This study was conducted in a rural section of New York where church life was not of a notably high quality in general and where the vast majority of the families of the children involved had no church connections. The potential value of the Church as a controlling influence, however, was recognized in the following quotation from a case history of one of the delinquent families involving the mother and daughters: "When Mrs. M. was ready to leave this institution at the end of a year, the parole officer, the home relief visitor, the county children's worker, *the minister of the church,* and a boarding mother who had cared for one of the younger children, all worked together to help her establish herself in the community. . . . The church to which they later claimed allegiance could at the time have given them spiritual strength and guidance in addition to a friendly interest."[2]

Using a 70-item test, George E. Hill compared the ethical knowledge of 517 delinquent boys to that of more than 1000 high school students and 148 adults and found very little difference between the scores of the offenders and the school group. A few single items showed marked differences, but the author felt that those differences were not large enough to be symptomatic of delinquency.[3]

Mathias measured the ideas of God held by 270 boys and girls (grades 5-8) from a "supposedly typical American population" and compared the scores with the findings of a character education study that had previously been made of the same group. He found fairly high positive correlations (statistical relationship) between the scores on his test and such items in the previous character study as moral knowledge, high motives, and parents' church membership, but low positive correlation between ideas of God and Sunday school attendance and honesty and co-operation. He believed, however, that while most correlations were low, taken together they give evidence of a positive relationship between God-ideas and conduct.[4]

Pleasant R. Hightower, in his University of Iowa studies in character, found no significant relationship between Biblical knowledge and conduct.[5] Hartshorn and May discovered no direct relationship between the Sunday school attendance (length of time and regularity) of children and their tendency to deceive. They warn, however, that too much weight should not be given to these facts.[6] Todd, in his thesis research on *Social Norms and the Behavior of College Students,* at Columbia University, reported that students who love people received high ratings in all areas of adjustments covered in his study and that religious students tend to make satisfactory adjustments in nearly all the areas. He concluded: "This indicates some tendency of religious values to integrate life toward successful adjustment."[7]

In his *Social Determinants in Juvenile Delinquency,* Sullenger expressed the conviction that "the Church with its various auxiliaries is also a potential force in preventing juvenile delinquency" and stated that his opinion could be substantiated by many testimonials from authoritative leaders. He cited statistics showing that of the 2191 cases studied by the Delinquency Committee of the White House Conference, only 27 per cent of the respondents attended Sunday school regularly; 26 per cent attended irregularly, while 37 per cent had no church connections.[8] Had statistics been available on Sunday school attendance by children in general in the communities from which the above cases were taken, there probably would not have been much difference, as the non-delinquent population attended only a little more regularly.

Lowell J. Carr, writing for the Michigan Juvenile Delinquency Information Service, observed that often social workers are very critical of the part that the Church has been taking in the delinquency prevention movement. But it was his opinion that the aid of churches is needed in any community delinquency control program if it takes the form of service rather than mere verbal idealism. He implied that the Church as the primary purveyor of ethical values might do more to aid in the realization of those values here and now by making religion truly functional in the community.[9] Austin L. Porterfield, who is, by his own admission, "an ardent churchman," found the churches doing all too little in making the ideals of

Jesus functional to the extent of acting as a preventive of delinquency. He reported that he knew of no study which showed that there are fewer delinquents in highly churched areas than where there are fewer churches. Yet he indicated a belief that the Church could and should do more to help youth and their parents with their specific and tangible needs, while continuing to carry out its all-important job of developing creative personality.[10]

These and other authorities vary widely in their findings and opinions regarding the value of the Church in preventing delinquency. That it could and ought to play a more significant role is generally expressed or intimated. Courts usually ascribe to it a greater significance than do social workers, who often serve as probation officers. This is illustrated in a study at the Judge Baker Guidance Clinic of the case records of 500 children placed on probation by the Juvenile Court of Boston. Instructions on the report card given by the court to the child state that "The Court has put you on probation to give you a chance to make good. You must do your best to succeed in school and at work, at home, in church or temple, and among your friends." On this card are nine rules on "How to Win on Probation," of which No. 8 is "Keep strictly your religious duties and win reverence and faith."[11]

Yet in discussing the probationary system, the author writes: "The social treatment conducted by the probation officer is concerned chiefly with five major phases of the child's life: (1) his home situation—the place and conditions under which he lives; (2) his physical and mental health; (3) the use of leisure time—his companions and recreational activities; (4) his education; and (5) his experience in earning a livelihood."[12]

The church life or religious life of the child is recognized in the study just cited as a positive factor, but to such a small extent that it is seldom mentioned and only as incidental to certain aspects of recreation and family life. It is not regarded as a major phase in the child's life or a dynamic force in his behavior, though the court evidently assumes that it is.

However varied the opinions of jurists, probation officers, and social workers, and whatever its failure has been in the past, the

Church believes itself to be the purveyor of a divine power that can transform human personality and stabilize human character. For nearly 2000 years it has been giving testimony to and evidence of such transformations, though the relative numbers affected may have been small. It may be charged that the Church has depended too much on exhortation and direct appeal and too little on an intelligent understanding of (1) the emotional forces that operate within the child and (2) the frustrating factors in the family and community situation that form emotional complexes and compulsive drives which prevent the growth of wholesome ideals and behavior patterns. The same charge may be made against the public school. Such knowledge is new and poorly disseminated.

Although the majority of local churches may have been ineffective in their dealings with problem children and with the family and neighborhood conditions that contribute to delinquency, the Church as a whole is vitally interested in this problem. Thousands of ministers, directors of Christian education, and youth workers are studying the inner forces and outer factors that make for delinquency, and thousands of local churches are reorganizing their total youth and children's programs in the light of this new knowledge. More and more churches and church leaders are turning their attention in the direction of the home, using the facilities of the Church, the dynamics of religion, and the insights of psychology to work toward more wholesome and creative family living. Church school curricula are being rewritten in terms of a family-centered, rather than a church-centered, emphasis; and churches are continually enlarging their local programs and camp activities to supplement family and community provisions for adequate living. Ministers and lay churchmen are serving as volunteer probation officers. These, in brief, are a few of the ways the Church is expressing its concern.

Whatever the degree of success or failure attained by the various churches in their youth and children's programs, these programs are increasing in scope. Churches are showing a growing concern regarding the problem of delinquency and child welfare and are searching for more effective means of meeting the challenge—for knowledge of how to make religion a more effective force in child and family life. This trend is reflected in the proceedings of the Mid-century White House Conference on Children and Youth, which met in December, 1950. One commentator observed that:

> . . . the midcentury event may be said to have been significant as symbolizing the need for co-operative planning on the part of the entire community for the welfare of every child, and for its recognition of the importance of religion in the child's life.
>
> Developments at this conference gave striking evidence that there is a return to religion among those who are concerned for the welfare of the 53,932,000 Americans under 21 years of age. Unlike preceding White House conferences, this one did not ignore the importance of fostering the spiritual aspect of the child's nature. That was given its place in the declared purpose of the conference: "To consider how we can develop in children the mental, emotional and spiritual qualities essential to individual happiness and to responsible citizenship, and what physical, economic and social conditions are deemed necessary to this development."[13]

Churches and churchmen have assumed that the good character goes with good religion and that religious activities should develop character. *If it has been revealed, as certain studies appear to show, that the Church has been relatively ineffective as a character-building or delinquency-preventing agency, the reason may be found in its methods rather than in the assumption that it has no great inherent value.* The problem of the local church as it relates to delinquency is to re-examine its program and redirect its activities so as to make religion function as a dynamic force in the home and early life of the child. To do that well its leaders must have much more knowledge of the role religion has been playing in the family life of delinquents and of its effectiveness or failure as a directing force toward wholesome living. The Church is gaining that knowledge.

Even Sheldon, who is most unorthodox if not outright negative in his attitude toward the Church, believes that organized religion can play a (possibly *the*) vital role in solving the problems of delinquency if it can shake off its theological delusions, forget the ideas of God and personal immortality, stop teaching children to worship, and concentrate its energy in such a manner as to become the chief protagonist of biological humanics.[14]

That the Church will discard its theology and institute the highly radical changes which Sheldon advocates is highly improbable. But that the Church will continue to study children and child behavior and to reorganize its program and revitalize its activities in its efforts to better serve children and youth is a practical certainty.

The Church has always been concerned with the problem of human character and behavior. The Gospel it has proclaimed, and which has been partly accepted by millions of people, has had a beneficial effect on behavior. The transformation of individual character and family relations where one or both parents were "converted" is an old and frequent experience in the life history of the Church. The ideals and standards it has held before society long have been among the forces that tend to prevent illegal and socially unacceptable behavior. And most of the character-building agencies of the community that combat delinquency more directly grew out of the Church. Furthermore, the spirit of concern for the problem child and family on the part of the public and private agencies for the prevention, care, and treatment of our erring and unfortunate children is largely a religiously inspired force.

However, the concern of the Church for your problem child—and the problem situations that aggravated his condition—has not been adequately expressed in terms of direct action. Now, in this generation, your Church has become cognizant of this neglect, is repentant, and is setting before itself the task of making up for its negligence. The Church is now moving rapidly to implement its concern with programs of specific action, based on years of study and deep understanding. Its spirit of concern has become embodied in agencies and activities that are both preventive and remedial. Church conferences, associations, etc., are conducting seminars for ministers and church lay leaders, exploring causes and forms of delinquency and agencies and methods of prevention and control, with special emphasis on the role of the Church and its relationship to other community agencies. Seminaries are exploring the problem to determine how best to train future ministers to meet it effectively. If yours or your neighbor's is a problem child or family, your church can help with the problem or guide you to a more specific source of help.

The Methodist Church at its 1952 General Conference authorized the establishment of a Board of Social and Economic Relations to become one of its major functional agencies. The Social Creed of the Methodist Church has long stood out as one of the great pronouncements of social concern. Realizing that it had been tardy in the implementation of its noble creed by an effective program of action, this denomination instituted the above board. "We do affirm the historic position of the Methodist Church of the right of its people to interpret the Christian faith in the field of social and economic relations and to work to bring our social order more nearly in accordance with the dictates of their own conscience."[15] One of the major activities of this board is to effect programs of action in the field of social welfare, particularly in the area of child and family welfare. It also operates directly in programs of action for improved housing, higher economic standards, and better living conditions for migrant workers and others of the lowest income brackets. Improved race relations comes in for a major share of its concern. In these and other activities the Methodist Church is seeking to reduce the tensions, conflicts, and frustrations that are conducive to delinquency.

The General Board of Social and Economic Relations works through similar boards in each of the more than one hundred Annual Conferences of the Methodist Church. These in turn are now helping to initiate the setting up of local church committees or commissions to study social and economic conditions and to co-operate with similar committees in other local churches and with other community agencies in the whole area of social concern. Many local churches already were sponsoring effective programs in this field—some of the larger with professional psychiatrists, counselors, or social workers in the church itself.

Far in advance of the Methodist Church in time and scope, the National Lutheran Council Division of Welfare, through its Lutheran Service Societies in most metropolitan centers, has developed the most widespread and effective social service program of any of the Protestant fellowships. Outstanding is the work of its institutional chaplains and its large staff (many staffs) of social caseworkers. Family and child welfare receive much of the attention of these trained workers. Work and play therapies are essential emphases. And placement of problem children in foster homes rather than in an institution, in so far as it is feasible or possible, is the present trend. *quote taken from Statement by*

Harold E. Hegstrom, Superintendent, National Training School for Boys, Washington, D.C., has stated the Lutheran concern for the delinquent child as effectively, perhaps, as any one person can. He writes:

> It is not sufficient to state that the church has an important role in the prevention of delinquency. The teachings of the church demand leadership and participation in a prevention program. Christ was the greatest social worker the world has seen and the Scriptures are full of his works. His whole life was one of social ministering. . . .
>
> The topic of the church in delinquency suggests four major thoughts that I would like to consider:
>
> 1. There is a mutual relation between the church and delinquency. The function of the church in the world is primarily spiritual; to make God a reality to men and to lead men to God. In establishing God as the alpha and omega of human life, it integrates a man's life and gives the deepest spiritual basis to his values. In the speculative order, his philosophy of life is rooted in the lasting eternal truths. In the practical order, these truths give him the best answer to his most difficult problems, genuine norms for good living. Delinquency is a revolt against authority and the moral law, especially in reference to man and society. It is the antithesis of what the church is trying to effect among men. The church and delinquency are then related as effort and failure. If the church perfectly accomplished its task there would be no delinquency. . . .
>
> 2. What should the church's attitude be toward delinquency? This question should call for a careful and honest self-examination. Is the church at fault for failing to reach the delinquent? . . . Examining the above question, we must admit that a

weakness exists and the only sincere procedure is to renew and reinforce the present efforts to reach the delinquent. This calls upon the church to prepare its leaders to bring the power and influence of the church to bear on the problem as it exists, and that they develop leaders and organizations to deal with all individuals and particularly those who are in imminent danger of becoming delinquents. The real church member will utilize his ability and efforts to become tolerant and friendly with those he can assist . . .

3. The church's part in the prevention of delinquency. If the church stands for anything, it stands for respect and authority. Delinquency is ultimately a denial of and revolt against authority. The Church represents the most fundamental authority of all, that of God and His divine Law. There is no law or authority in human society which does not ultimately derive from the law and authority of God. Hence, by stressing this fundamental authority . . . the church is forwarding the basis of an ordered social life, the opposite of delinquency. . . . The Church should make every effort to rid the urban areas of its slums, and of fighting subnormal economic conditions. Leadership is needed to prevent discord in the home, divorce and promiscuity, broken homes, and infidelity. The church could do well to take its stand on eliminating immoral books, obscene literature, questionable movies, fantastic literature and radio programs that foster disorders in moral life and thus foster delinquency, especially in the case of impressionable young people. While the church must consider seriously these negative factors that I have just mentioned, the church must have a positive attitude toward building up and supporting Christian institutions which can develop the stable family life, good education, wholesome recreational facilities, youth groups, clubs, labor unions for a living wage, co-operatives for lower prices. Anything that fosters the living of a well-ordered life is a good insurance against delinquency, and prevention is always better and cheaper than cure.

4. This leads us to the fourth point: the treatment of delinquency. Fundamentally, the establishment of the above program will stand as a long-range cure for delinquency. The immediate problem is an interest in the delinquent himself and in

his rehabilitation, both in the institution and on release. The church represents the Saviour in the world. He came to save all, and certainly the delinquent is in great need of salvation. The first fruit of Calvary was the penitent thief . . . In the institution, the chaplain needs the support of other members of the church; his work is more difficult when he feels that he is alone in it. Even with help, it is difficult. He must re-orientate the delinquent. Rigid discipline will never bring about the change in attitude. The chaplain must offer real friendship and patient interest necessary to sustain Christian principles. The chaplain and the church must be close to the delinquent if he is to remake his life. If they are with him, he will be reassured and encouraged in this difficult task. The delinquent encounters the most difficult phase of his life upon leaving the institution, and it is here the church must take up where the chaplain leaves off. Many do not understand the delinquent's problems and the difficulties of beginning life anew. If the church and his fellow church members do not understand him and help him return to normal life, there is little chance for rehabilitation.[16]

Other of the larger Protestant fellowships are following close behind the Lutheran groups. The Roman Catholic Church, through its "Catholic Charities," has been ministering for years to its problem families and problem children with a well-organized program of social casework, counseling, and institutional care.

Elaine Holcomb, wife of a Southern Baptist minister and a leader in United Church Women, recently completed her Master's Thesis on *The Role of Religion in the Prevention of Juvenile Delinquency*. The fact that Mrs. Holcomb, in order to implement her religious concern, majored in sociology of religion and did her research and thesis in the field of delinquency is in itself an indication of the growing Southern Baptist concern. This interest is further indicated by the wide distribution of a leaflet entitled, "The Christian's Attitude Toward Delinquency," by the Home Mission Board, Southern Baptist Convention, suggesting practical ways the local church can aid in prevention of delinquency.

(1) Develop a strong Christian program in slum and other neglected areas, by establishing Good Will Centers, preaching points, or mission stations.

(2) Enlist the support of church groups to provide an immediate ministry of love, sympathy, and concern to the home broken by death, divorce, desertion, or any other type of disruptive force.

(3) Make possible summer camperships or camp scholarships to children who otherwise would be denied the opportunities offered by a Christian summer camp.

(4) Enlist every unenlisted child in the life of the church, remembering that seldom does an active member of the Sunday school or church find his way into the court.

(5) Develop a "Fellowship Hour" by making available to the unenlisted homes of the community a program of Christian fellowship.

(6) Co-operate with the evangelistic committee and pastor of the church in a special effort to win the families that have presented some particular problem in the community.

(7) Give particular attention to the downtown areas where churches have moved out, leaving no type of spiritual ministry behind, allowing the forces of evil to move in unsuppressed.

(8) Extend the outreach of Christian love to families of children who are involved in trouble.

(9) Extend fullest support to every agency seeking to help delinquent children and their families.

(10) Urge young persons contemplating marriage to seek a conference with the pastor, where an opportunity for Christian counseling may prepare them for a Christian home and permanent marriage.[17]

Mrs. Holcomb made an exhaustive study of published statements by church leaders, psychologists, and social scientists relative to the role of religion and churches in character building and delinquency prevention. She also corresponded with denominational and interdenominational leaders relative to planned and promoted activities in their special area. Her work being so up-to-date, with her permission I shall quote extensively from her findings. She writes:

In a consultation on November 5, 1954, regarding Christian Education and Childhood Delinquency sponsored by the Departments of Pastoral Services and Children's Work of the National Council of Churches it was brought out that the church needs to learn how to deal with children with anxiety aroused by a conflict between values learned in the home, community and the church, because it is "relying too much on verbal teaching when the child learns otherwise."

Even though it is the consensus of opinion of most social scientists and laymen that churches are needed in community efforts of delinquency control, some might wonder what churches are doing about this matter. Sociologist Vedder claims that the Catholic Church and such Protestant denominations as the American Baptist, the Protestant Episcopal, various Lutheran Churches and the Congregational Christian Church have "sponsored programs designed to curb delinquency." This present investigation has received data from these Protestant Churches indicating such efforts on their part as well as from the Southern Baptists and the Presbyterian Church, U.S.A. A letter from the Department of Church and Community Service of the Disciples of Christ indicated that it is prepared to hold Church and Community Clinics on Delinquency and its causes. . . . Another evidence of churches' growing concern for community welfare is that one of the mission themes interdenominationally for the year 1955 was "The City." Materials were prepared at all age levels on "The City" and one of the chief filmstrips, "City Story," was concerned largely with the matter of delinquency.

Theological seminaries also realize the church's obligation to the community and are offering courses to future ministers and religious educational leaders that will equip them in administering to the communities of which their churches will be a part. A letter from a seminary professor indicates this trend in seminary training by stating: "We offer a course also in community life in which the agencies designed to improve and support family life in the community are interested. It is not our intention to relax the historic Baptist emphasis upon the dignity and worth of the individual, but we want our students to understand that the individual grows toward maturity in a family, that the family lives in a community, and that the community is vitally related to the regional culture. We think the church and the pastor have an opportunity to participate in the building of the kind of community that will prevent juvenile delinquency and encourage growth of children and youth toward Christian maturity."

Other denominations are doing outstanding work in working with youth in underprivileged areas of cities. Two examples of such work are found in the McKim Center in Baltimore, Maryland, and the Cameron House in San Francisco. Both are sponsored by the Presbyterian Church, U.S.A. Another type of work that can be regarded as a means toward delinquency prevention is the church-related organizations within the Episcopal Church, which do work with adolescents. These organizations are Girls' Friendly Society in New York, Order of Sir Galahad in Boston, Junior Daughters of the King in New York, and the Brotherhood of St. Andrew in York, Pennsylvania.

An example of an outstanding program of a church in a slum area can be found in the Church of All Nations in Los Angeles, established thirty years ago by the Methodist Church. It is located in the worst section of that city which has the highest crime rate for adults in the country. This church has included a variety of health and welfare units and has endeavored in many ways to be a "trusted friend of the families, the children and young people of the east side." These efforts have resulted in an 83 per cent reduction in juvenile delinquency since the founding of this church.[18]

In Protestantism, the Church's concern is perhaps most effectively expressed through Councils of Churches. At national, state, and county levels these Councils have organized departments through which this concern is expressed. While the specific names of these departments and the exact nature of the programs vary in different Councils, all are prepared to work for a better adjustment of problem children in their respective families and communities. Some maintain direct counseling service to help disturbed children and parents work out their problems. Some operate a chaplaincy service and/or support social workers at institutions and courts who handle cases of youth offenders and domestic problems. All provide a referral service designed to direct the local church and family to the best available sources of help for their problem children.

Yes, your Church is concerned with your problem and is taking rapid strides toward effective implementation of that concern—from its national organization right down to the local congregation. Its years of study and experimentation have provided the necessary knowledge. Thus it can speak with authority and serve effectively in areas of family and social adjustment.

4

The Problem Child
Is Religious

THE CONCERN OF THE CHURCH FOR ITS PROB-
LEM CHILDREN is matched by their interest in the Church. They
believe in God and the Bible and the Church and have positive
religious convictions, but they are confused religiously and socially.
Often they are adept at keeping their religious interests camouflaged
from others, sometimes from themselves. But at the heart of them
—when you get into their hearts and the heart of their problem—
they are believers and sincerely religious.

A look back at chapter 1 will reveal the general religious attitudes
and feelings of a great many delinquent children. Bob was largely
neutral and confused in his thinking. During earlier childhood he
had been quite religious and enjoyed the Sunday school and religious
activities of his home. It was only after several years of conflict,
frustration, and disillusion that he turned slightly sour on religion
and cut himself off from the Church. Even then he was more positive
than negative in his religious attitudes, believed in God and the
value of the Bible and the Church, but had largely lost hope that
religion could be of much help to him.

Belle, in spite of much conflict, misunderstanding, and the poor
exemplification of religion by her mother, was still sincerely and
deeply religious. She was a church member and thought of herself
as being Christian. Conflict, resentment, and other emotional forces
which she did not understand resulted in confused religious feelings,
some guilt, and some periods of felt alienation from God. But she

held to her belief in Christ and His redeeming power and continued to seek it for herself. Fay, like Belle, was quite firm in her positive religious convictions. With no encouragement from her father and encouragement of a mixed value from her mother, she attended Sunday school and church more or less regularly (regular in periods and lax at other periods), received instructions for membership, and joined a church. Her attitudes, too, were strongly positive, and her feelings frequently confused, with periodic feelings of alienation from God. Yet she felt herself to be Christian, believed implicitly in the value of religion, and recognized its partial failure in her case as being due to the family conflict situation and her teen-age neglect to cultivate her religious life.

George, who grew up under extremely unwholesome family conditions and who had thereby developed psychopathic traits, was responding from behind such a rigid defense system that his religious attitudes and feelings were largely neutral. Theoretically he believed in the general value of religion but it left him basically untouched at the inner citadel of his life. Yet, even he was receptive in so far as his inner defenses permitted, having "read the Bible through while in jail . . . ," and he might well have been more deeply responsive under the guidance of a pastor-counselor who could have helped him work through his defenses to a deeper self-awareness and self-acceptance. Irvin's responses were not far different from those of Bob—a little more positive and a little more mixed or confused. He believed in God and the Church, and in the general value of religion in life. And he realized that circumstantial factors, more than any inherent fault of religion or the Church, accounted for the relative failure of religion as a positive force in his own life.

While these five young people reflect typical religious attitudes and feelings, they are not statistically representative. Two of these five were members of churches and strongly positive in their attitudes. Of the thirty youngsters studied intensively by the writer, eleven were members of churches and thought themselves to be average or above in Christian character, though conscious of their imperfections and inability to cope with their frustrating circumstances—their occasional "messing up" without knowing just why, or how to prevent it. Only five thought of themselves as not being Christian at all. Let us look more fully at one of these, a very bitter boy.

Regis was a 17-year-old white boy, stockily built, of low-medium height, and athletic in appearance. While talking to the writer he would answer direct questions in an apparently honest, matter-of-fact sort of monotone, but he never came out fully from behind his defenses.

He lived in the outskirts of a small city in a neighborhood that was, in his words, "not too good; not too bad." He was the second youngest of nine children, and his parents were living together. The father, though a moderately heavy drinker, provided for the material needs of the family. They were poor but not in a state of poverty. Case records showed that three of his father's near relatives had criminal records. When Regis was 12 years old, he and some other boys stole some trinkets from a store, but charges against them were not pressed. About a year later he was involved in a case of property damage. For this and truancy he was sent to a special school for younger delinquents. His adjustment there was satisfactory and he was released after 20 months. While at home he worked at odd jobs but found no steady work. With too much leisure time and not enough money or supervision, he began to loaf at questionable places with a "gang" of older boys. They were charged with several burglaries and convicted; and Regis was sent to another school for delinquents, though he stoutly denied any major part in the misdemeanors. He was merely with them, he claimed, on a couple of occasions, took no part in the burglaries, and could not have prevented them.

He was deeply resentful of his committal and felt that society was against him, that his punishment was too severe for his minor mistakes. This feeling was intensified a few months after commitment when he was accused of stealing a ring and a cigarette lighter, removed from his job at the institution's tailor shop, and given a less favorable job. He denied the charge and was bitterly resentful, engaged in frequent fights, seldom smiled, was regarded as surly, adjusted to a minimum degree (just sufficient to stay out of trouble), often muttered threats, and constantly lived within his defense shell.

Regis reported both on the test and on the interview that his parents had no religious interest, that there was no religious training or activity in the home, and that only his mother attended church, and she seldom. He and the other children attended Sunday school occasionally but had no part in other church activities, and he stopped going to Sunday school altogether by the time he was nine or ten. He reported a belief in the existence of God but had serious doubts at times. He made no pretense of being a Christian or trying to be one. He would not attend chapel (at the school) if it were not compulsory, and he reportedly paid no attention. His religious feelings, as best he could describe them, were consistently neutral except for occasional feelings of confusion and alienation. He had "nothing against the Church or Bible . . . just not interested in them. They are of some value but not to me." Thus he was not antagonistic, and showed a mildly positive attitude by what he was not against, even though consciously he was indifferent.

Officers at the school believed that at the best Regis could have been developed into a fine boy; at worst, he could deteriorate into a very dangerous one. His general code of ethics was satisfactory, and he was basically honest and trustworthy. His major problem was one of deep resentment against his lot in life—against society for being too hard on him and always suspicious of him, and against his family for the stigma that was partly responsible for "people being against me."

The case of Regis is typical of the very small percentage of delinquents who were found to be negative or neutral toward the Church and religion. He would have been difficult for the average church to hold, but a church had the opportunity. And a church and community functioning as will be described in chapters 7 and 8 might well have prevented his committals or brought about a satisfactory adjustment to society after the first one.

But our interest in this chapter is to show that the large majority of our problem children are religious and can be reached by the Church. Kate illustrates this majority attitude. She was a 17-year-old white girl, slender and nervous, but friendly and talkative, frequently displaying a wry smile. The youngest of three children, with less than 18 months between the births of any two of them, she was worried about the brother next to her in age, who had just been released from a school for delinquents, fearing that he might get into trouble again. Kate was also worried about her mother, talked at length about her, and hoped that she would become a Christian.

There was much quarreling at home during her early childhood. The father drank a lot, and the mother "a little." The quarreling centered mostly in the mother's "chasing around." Apparently the father was jealous of the mother and had sufficient grounds. She was "out" frequently, leaving the children alone or with a neighbor, and left home for periods of several days on three different occasions. Kate's paternal grandmother reported that the mother was "no good and never was," that she always chased around with other men and neglected the children. The grandmother took the oldest child at the age of 16 months, when the second child was born, and has kept him since.

At the age of eight Kate was seriously injured by an auto while playing in the street. Plastic surgery was provided; but a large scar remained to disfigure her face, and this apparently affected her personality. When she was eleven, her parents separated permanently. Kate lived with an uncle and aunt for a while but couldn't get along with them. She was placed in two foster homes for short periods, then was back with her mother and "stepfather" for a while. A year was spent in an orphanage, but Kate didn't like it there, ran away, and was committed to a girls' training school. Stealing, lying, and temper tantrums were the symptoms of her problem.

Institutional records described her as a thin, pale, anxious child, immature, frequently moody, unpopular, not inclined to play, fond of dancing and singing, and sincere in her religious convictions. She tried to get other girls to be better Christians (becoming a nuisance at times) and suffered hurt feelings when they ridiculed her. Her I.Q. reports ranged from 87 to 110.

Interviews and test scores indicated very little religious interest or activity in Kate's childhood home. Her father showed some interest and attended church occasionally, but there was no home worship or religious training. Interview and test reports were in complete harmony. Kate attended Sunday school and said her prayers occasionally during early childhood.

There appeared to be a great change in religious activity during the adolescent period. This sudden change began when she lived with her grandparents. She became active in attendance at various church functions, including the youth choir, was instructed in the Catechism, and joined a Lutheran church at the age of 13. She reported a conversion experience at the age of 15. Test and interview revealed strongly positive religious attitudes, occasional confused feelings, and occasional feelings that her prayers were unanswered. These negative feelings were usually associated with her depressed moods. She reported infrequent doubts as to the existence of God, rated herself as a better than average Christian, thought of Jesus as her best friend and prayer as "making me feel closer to God." She found no fault in her church but stated that she had no home religious training. "If I had I wouldn't be here," she said.

Kate is a girl whose chief trouble apparently is based on feelings of rejection by her mother, a lack of love during childhood. Yet she yearns for her mother, and, in a measure, associates herself with her mother, sharing in her guilt. The stealing was, no doubt, a compulsive substitute response for a lack of love. Any church with a vital youth program and counseling service could have helped Kate solve her basic problem and make a good social adjustment.

More will be said about the home conditions of the problem child in the next chapter, but certain facts are presented here to show that religious interest exists in the homes from which these children come, giving rise to much of their interest in religion. Two-thirds of the young people studied by the writer—a sampling that was representative of the entire Protestant delinquent population of a large metropolitan area—reported that one or both of their parents were members of a church. A little more than one-third were from homes where both parents were members, leaving slightly less than one-third from homes where neither parent was a church member. Some of the faults of these homes will be pointed out later, faults partly recognized by the children. However, nearly three-fourths of these teen-age delinquents rated their homes as average or better. Twenty per cent thought there was some Christianity shown but not much, while only 5.6 per cent rated their homes as being totally lacking in Christian influence.

While these young people were evidently too generous in their appraisal of the religious quality of their homes, such factors being highly subjective, personal interviews with many of them and their parents showed them to be 90 to 95 per cent accurate in objective data reported. Thus it was quite evident that not many of them were reared in homes that had no trace of Christian influence. Christianity, at least to some degree, was recognized by the majority of these delinquent young people as a factor in their family life. *Their homes were not closed to the Church.*

Furthermore, the majority of these parents sent their children to Sunday school and church and provided some religious training in their homes. Eighty-five per cent of the group reported regular or occasional Sunday school attendance, leaving only 15 per cent who attended seldom or never. Over 60 per cent observed bedtime prayers regularly and an additional 20 per cent occasionally. Less than 10 per cent reported that they had never engaged in the practice of prayer at bedtime.

Religion as a dynamic factor in one's life can be observed in part, at least, by the extent to which the religious activities and interests of early childhood continue through the intermediate years into adolescence. The reported drop in Sunday school attendance during the intermediate years was a little more than 12 per cent, reaching 33 per cent between early and mid-adolescence—the drop being based on the change from regular to occasional and from occasional to seldom or never. Fourteen was the average age when most who discontinued Sunday school dropped out. This was the age when in most cases conflict was becoming intense and problem symptoms well-established. However, in spite of the problem-producing factors in the homes and communities, more than half of these problem children had joined churches, one-third of them had received training in church membership or the Catechism, and one in five reported a conversion experience. The writer was surprised to find that three-

fourths of the group continued the habit of prayer regularly or occasionally.

That problem children are religious is indicated quite clearly by
their church activities, but religion is something more than mere
activity. How do they feel and think with respect to religion—these
young people with the stigma of social misbehavior attached to their
names, cut off from normal society, and confined to the regimented
life of an institution? What do they believe about Jesus, prayer, and
their own religious training? What are their attitudes toward the
Church, the Bible, and God? To find answers to some of these
questions, they were questioned about their prayer habits, feelings
of forgiveness or lack of it, feelings of God's presence, of wanting
to be helpful, of help in making decisions, feelings of confusion, of
alienation, etc. The answers presented do not give an accurate, objective measure of religious feelings—a most difficult, if not impossible, thing to do—but do provide some measure of their continuing
interests and responses. These feelings and attitudes were characteristic of their period of conflict and commitment.

That 48 per cent reported frequent experiences of forgiveness
following prayer is not of primary importance, such statistical exact-
ness being impossible. The significant fact is that a majority of these
young people continued the habit of prayer and believed that it
helped them. More than three-fourths of them reported the belief
that out of their worship experiences they received help in making
decisions and that they had feelings of wanting to be helpful to
others. Feelings of confusion characterized more than half of the
group and a sense of alienation from God was reported by one-third
of them.

Approximately three-fourths of these troubled children had no
serious doubt regarding the existence of God, while 5 per cent reported complete disbelief. The others fluctuated between belief and
disbelief, disbelieving mostly when upset. Belief and action, however,
are different things. The ideational and functional elements in
religion never quite keep pace. Though notably generous in their
self-appraisal, as they were in the appraisal of their homes, these
disturbed youngsters recognized this disparity to a limited degree.

The majority rated themselves as average or above in their own Christian living, but only 4 per cent thought of themselves as being among the best Christian young people and a little more than one-third rated themselves as being not Christian at all or Christian to a very small degree. Furthermore, after making justifiable allowances for the tendency to overrate, both test questions and personal interviews revealed that approximately three-fourths of the group sincerely believed that their faith in God had a beneficial influence on them. They not only believed in God but believed that He influenced their lives for good. The belief in the influence of God in their lives closely paralleled their self-rating as Christians and ran well behind their reported belief in the existence of God. While a more objective rating of the Christian quality of the character of these young people would undoubtedly be lower than their own self-rating, the significant fact is that they think of themselves as being Christian and are thus within the sphere of the Church's influence, even though they "keep messing up," often not knowing why.

If the Church is to play a key role in helping the problem child solve his basic problem, which the writer believes it can and ought to do, we of the Church should know how they feel toward the Church and the Bible. Have they developed a cynical attitude toward the Church and lost confidence in the teachings of the Bible? By test questions and personal interviews this information was sought. With a carefully developed system for doublechecking responses on two parallel forms to catch serious inconsistencies, it was found that 68 per cent of the respondents held strongly positive attitudes toward the Church, 19 per cent held mildly positive attitudes, 8 per cent were neutral, and 5 per cent were either mildly or strongly antagonistic. Attitude responses toward the Bible followed a closely similar pattern. Without arguing that these statistics are 100 per cent reliable, it is evident that the Church still has a hold on the minds of a vast majority of these delinquent young people. And in the Bible, if properly used, it has a valuable instrument for its work with them. Furthermore, there was not a great difference between the attitudes of the boys and girls, although the latter ran somewhat more strongly positive.

Quite often check lists of statements are suggestive and may not yield results that reflect the true attitudes of the respondents. To correct any misapprehensions at this point, this group of delinquent children were asked both on the test and in personal interviews, after rapport had been well established, to state in their own words how they thought or felt about Jesus, prayer, the good and bad points of their churches, and how they felt about their home training in religion. Questions regarding Jesus brought such orthodox and fundamentalistic answers as these in approximately 60 per cent of the cases: "He is the Son of God"; "true God"; "Saviour"; "giver of eternal life"; "I love Him"; "believe all the Bible says about Him"; "He means everything to me"; "is all the world to me"; "is my ideal." Another 30 per cent expressed soundly Christian, though somewhat more liberal and humanistic, views in such statements as these: "He is the only one to turn to in trouble"; "helps one to know God"; "helps one to get along"; "watches over you"; "helps the sick"; "He is a great man"; "a great prophet"; "the most perfect man"; "like a hero or father of our country." Only 2 per cent were indifferent or negative in their responses, replying that: "He means little"; "never gave Him much consideration"; "I don't believe in Him"; "no interest in Him"; "He means nothing." Ninety per cent of these problem children reportedly believe in Jesus, are Christian in their attitude toward Him; and face-to-face conversation with them convinced the writer that they were largely sincere.

To the questions "Do you believe prayer helps?" and "If so, how?", only 15 per cent held serious doubt or outright disbelief—answering in such terms as "I don't know"; "it hasn't helped me much"; "no"; "I don't think so." A fourth of them showed unquestioning confidence in the efficacy of prayer, replying that "God answers prayer"; "prayer comes true"; "prayer helps"; "it helps to pray for others." The others, composing three out of every five, answered in terms of specific values that are derived through prayer. These expressed values can be generalized as peace of mind, inner strength, moral insight, and help in conduct. One youngster expressed a somewhat unusual insight, though similarly reflected by a few others, in the statement: "It helps me just to express myself to God."

As to how their church or Sunday school had helped them, replies were quite varied. A little over one-fifth of them were unspecific, saying "a lot" or "a little" or "in many ways." About 17 per cent replied: "It doesn't seem to help"; "it hasn't helped"; "none"; or "in no way." More than 60 per cent felt that church or Sunday school attendance produced such specific values as providing knowledge about God, the Bible, and how to live; increasing faith in or drawing one closer to God and Christ; helping to improve behavior (various forms specified); helping "to get saved."

Furthermore, the majority had no specific faults of the Church in mind. There was nothing they could think of that they held against it. Thus they were conscious of no specific barriers that would prevent their affiliation with it. The approximately 40 per cent who had specific criticisms to offer felt that their churches were noisy, lacking in order, boring, uninteresting, tiring, gossipy, or always after money; that they didn't teach the most important things or that things were not explained sufficiently; that the members interfered, meddled, were unfriendly, clannish, or played bingo. A few felt that the Church was "all right for some people" but not for them.

The questions regarding what they liked or disliked most about their home religious training, the largest single group were unable to answer on the grounds that there wasn't enough of it to evaluate. Some, of course, just couldn't be bothered by trying. However, of the nearly 60 per cent who did discuss these questions freely and critically, Bible stories and Bible reading and discussion were the most popular forms of home religious activity. Bedtime prayers, grace at table, and teaching of right from wrong followed in descending order. A large majority expressed the feeling that there was nothing wrong with the religious training given in their homes, but that there simply wasn't enough, some specifying the insufficiency of the above elements. One boy was very much "put out" about his home training because "We didn't sing enough." Another felt that the chief value of religious activities in the home was that "It brought members of our family together."

In Mrs. Holcomb's study of 200 delinquent boys and girls in Texas, using the same procedure this writer used in his earlier study, findings were strikingly similar to the above. Her problem children did not rate themselves, the Christian quality of their homes, and the influence of God in their lives as highly as did mine. But these are highly subjective factors, with no established criteria by which to rate accurately. Perhaps the Texas children were more realistic, or possibly Mrs. Holcomb interpreted the questions more clearly. Also, the percentage of Texas children who had joined churches was higher—67 per cent against 56 per cent in Pennsylvania. This can be accounted for partly by the fact that the Texas study included some Catholic children, all of whom are "church members," and by regional differences in normal age for joining church. On the whole, however, the general pattern of religious interests, attitudes, and activities were quite similar in both groups; also the religious features of their homes were strikingly similar.

Mrs. Holcomb found that:

(1) In about 75 per cent of the homes of the respondents, parents have shown some attempts at attending church.

(2) There is a definite lack of interest on the part of the parents toward active participation within the organization of the church.

(3) There is a noticeable lack of religious literature in the homes of the respondents—found in only one-third of the homes.

(4) There is little religious training in the homes, but a great desire on the part of many of the respondents for such training.

(5) Churches have had some contact with over three-fourths of the respondents; two-thirds of the respondents claim church membership and slightly over three-fourths of them claim regular or occasional attendance at Sunday school and church, particularly in early childhood.

. . . . . .

(11) Positive attitudes toward the Church, the Bible, and Jesus, and positive beliefs in the existence of God seem to indi-

> cate a tacit acceptance of the values of God, the Bible,
> Jesus, and the Church.[1]

These problem young people of ours—of our churches, our communities, our homes—are basically religious. A large majority of them are orthodox and somewhat uncritical in their thinking. They find value in prayer and in church attendance and are cognizant of the inadequacy of their home training. Win their confidence and they will drop their masks and reveal as much to you. This fact places the Church in the position of playing a key role in helping them solve their problems and thus avoiding delinquency. Why has it failed in so many cases to do this? Why did the religion of these troubled youth fail to support them adequately in the crisis? How can the Church play its role more adequately? Much research will be required to answer these questions in full, but they can now be answered in part.

Keeping in mind the fact that there are ten, twenty, or more children in your city or town who have more or less serious emotional and behavior problems for every one who is charged in court with delinquency and committed to an institution, it can be stated categorically that their religious convictions and the churches that foster them are preventive factors. But when conflict and frustration become too prolonged and severe, religion as a control over behavior breaks down and they find themselves "messing up" without fully understanding why. The accumulated resentments and aggressive feelings become stronger drives than their religious convictions can control. Any young person may, and most do, reach such a point at some time. The problem is one of type and degree of rebellion or misbehavior. Their problems being more difficult than those of most teeners, potential delinquents or neurotics need more personal counseling and a more vital group program.

The religious lives of these delinquent young people may be characterized as ideationally strong but functionally weak. They are positive in their religious attitudes and orthodox in their beliefs, but their behavior is often at wide variance with their ideals. This variance they recognize to a large degree though not fully. These problem kids do not stand alone in this. It strikes us all. But the characteristic is marked in them. We need to provide for them a more realistic and creative type of Christian education that draws out of the child's own growing emotional experiences the religious concepts he retains. Right ideas had been transmitted to their minds and had been accepted uncritically by them, but their concepts and convictions were shallow-rooted and their deeper emotional drives left largely unaffected. They needed personal help in learning how to worship effectively—how to respond to God and people at the deeper emotional levels. Most of them by late childhood and early adolescence had developed emotional complexes of hate, anxiety, insecurity, inferiority, and guilt, and were more than normally blocked and deficient in their emotional, and thus worship, responses. Faith and love could not develop normally under these conditions and were not strong enough to support them in their crises. Church educators are becoming cognizant of this situation and are progressing rapidly in gearing Christian education to this need. Continuing progress in this area of church activity means an increasingly effective role played by the Church to prevent delinquency and mental illness.

5.

The Church
and Our Homes

WE DO NOT LIKE TO BE CALLED A COMMUNIST nor have it inferred that we in any manner resemble one. Yet in our family living we in America appear to be following closely the Communistic party line. This is the introductory theme of chapter 1 in Elton and Pauline Trueblood's book, *The Recovery of Family Life*: "The sobering truth is that, in our conception of the family and its place in a total society, we are producing, without considered and conscious intent, much that the Russian planners have achieved by deliberate ideological emphasis. We are doing by neglect much that the Marxists have done by social planning."[1] This theme is developed through several pages; then they write:

> The tide of ideological fashion seems still to be moving in the direction of universal employment outside the home. It is not uncommon to find great factory and commercial establishments where there are more female than male employees. There are the so-called "chicken farms," offices in which endless rows of women are busy pecking away all day long. The sight is somehow very depressing. *En masse* they seem desexed, like the workers in the beehive. They are potential queens who have missed their vocation. Each *could* be pictured at the center of a home, making an island of peace and order in the confusion and strain of our day, but instead she runs an adding machine or files addresses in a noisy room filled with women.
>
> The chain of disaster is clear. The homes devoid of regular or continuous care lead directly to insecurity and delinquency

on the part of the young. These in turn set up homes where a
similar pattern is demonstrated. How shall we break this vicious
chain? Before we can break it we need to know the nature of
the trouble. Part of the trouble is, of course, economic, but by
no means all. A good share of the trouble is moral and, if we
go beyond the surface, most of it may be. One of the chief
reasons why so many habitations are not homes is that other
things are prized more. . . .

Part of the trouble lies in the fact that so much of the idea
of sanctity is gone. Easy divorce and quick remarriage, after the
Nevada model, mean that marriage is seen primarily as a private
convenience rather than a sacred undertaking.

C. C. Zimmerman, in his Harvard study, *Family and Civilization,* perhaps the most thorough work of the kind now in
existence, puts the matter tersely when he says, "In other words
the family is considered *de facto,* a private contract of a very
brittle nature and as having not even a mild public significance."
It ought to be clear that the present withering of the family is
exactly what we should expect in the light of the absence of a
generally accepted philosophy which would support the sanctity of marriage. The people who rush to Reno are not doing the
surprising thing; they are doing the wholly natural thing, given
their presuppositions. It is at this point that Zimmerman's analysis is both helpful and clear. "The religious and moral agents,"
he writes, "which once supported their systems of familism are
largely out of favor with the masses or are inwardly corrupted
by lack of knowledge of their real functions in society."

The secular atomism of the modern family makes three fundamental mistakes. First, it sees marriage as mere contract, second,
it understands marriage as a private affair, and third, it adopts
a philosophy of self-expression and empty freedom which rules
out the claims of self-sacrifice and self-control.[2]

The Truebloods end the chapter with the more optimistic outlook,
saying,

> Fortunately, there are still thousands, perhaps millions of
> good families in America where the bonds of affection are
> kept strong, but not even these are free from the danger

of the withering processes around them. Only by vigilance can the valued life we already have be kept and only by careful thought can its scope be increased. As the major threat to the life of the family lies in our ideas and convictions, so it is in this same area that our hope for a better future likewise lies. Can we recover or produce a conception of family life so intrinsically appealing that it makes us dissatisfied with the withering of the family in either the Russian or the Western style? That we *can* is the thesis of this book. . . .[3]

That the Church can play the most vital role of any agency in the enlargement and enrichment of family life, and thus in the prevention of delinquency, is the theme of this chapter. *The Church has the only adequate philosophy of family life. It is the conveyor of a divine dynamic by the aid of which this philosophy or ideal can be effected in family living. And it has access to the family as no other agency has.*

When we add defectiveness and perversion of family living to withering away as presented by the Truebloods, we have the major causative factors in delinquency. In a pamphlet entitled *Our Delinquent Children,* by C. Logan Landrum, the following opinions and findings are presented:

> While we must not unduly minimize other factors the one that probably plays the largest part in the formation of undesirable behavior patterns is the home, especially the intimate relationship of the delinquent to the different members of the family. In a thorough study of 259 case histories we found only three cases where home conditions were not listed as a possible factor in causing the delinquent behavior.
>
> It has been pointed out repeatedly that the fundamental needs of the child are two, namely: the need for security, that is to be loved and wanted, and the need for development. It is when these needs are unmet or when the child is thwarted in his attempt to meet them that he launches out upon a career of delinquency in order to find that which has been denied him in his home life.
>
> In our study of the records of local delinquents we found repeatedly that the delinquent was in a state of confusion and per-

plexity because of conflicts with his parents, his guardian, or with other members of his family. . . . Such perplexity as often exists in the mind of the child not only denies him the right to the satisfaction which comes from having his fundamental needs properly met but destroys his confidence in the home and its standards.

Another type of home is often found where the child is not always the object of the upheaval in the home but where the parents are constantly in conflict with one another, and the child, disappointed at the conduct of his parents and denied the proper satisfaction of his fundamental needs, forsakes it for the street, the gang and other substitute relationships.[4]

Dr. Landrum discussed parental neglect as a factor. Then writing on the character of parents he says:

One of the really important phases of the influence of the home upon delinquency is the effects of delinquent or vicious parents upon the juvenile delinquent. The very knowledge that his own father or mother is a law breaker can have a tremendous effect upon the child. If his love and respect for his parents were very strong it might cause him to lose all regard for the sacredness of the law, and to feel that there is no reason why he should observe it. On the other hand, it can have just the opposite effect of causing him to lose respect for his parents and thus to lose his sense of security.

. . . . . .

Of the several forms of parental failings that so severely affect the lives of Macon [Ga.] juvenile delinquents that of immorality is the commonest, not less than 31 per cent of white delinquents coming from homes where one or both parents were known to be immoral.

One of the most important angles to this problem is that of the atmosphere surrounding such homes. In several of the cases where the mother was the offending party a very undesirable environment has been created in the home by bringing in vicious characters whose influence upon the children cannot but be adverse. . . .

. . . . . .

Alcoholism also plays a prominent part in the lives of the parents of the subjects of our study. Of the white delinquents 48 per cent come from homes where one or both parents were found to be alcoholic. In some cases not only were both parents found to be alcoholic but the children as well. A study made by the Children's Bureau of 2,371 children in Boston, and reported by the White House Conference, found that 41 per cent of the fathers, 7 per cent of the mothers, and 6 per cent of the families both father and mother had been alcoholic at some time. Alcoholism then, is very common among the parents of delinquents not only here but in other localities. Some authorities report that alcoholism is almost three times as common among the families of delinquents as among those of non-delinquents.[5]

The writer's research in this field has yielded findings similar to those of Dr. Landrum, though the percentages of immoral and alcoholic parents were not as large as in his.

The local church has a unique opportunity to reach and enrich the family relationships of problem homes. For, by and large, the parents of our problem children are not irreligious or antagonistic to the Church. The minister or church worker is a welcomed visitor in the vast majority of these homes. He does not have to wait until invited but is free to visit any home, and he can tactfully bring the influence of his church to bear upon any problem discovered to exist there. Of the 150 inmates of schools for delinquents studied by the writer, approximately two-thirds came from homes where at least one parent was a church member. Slightly more than one-third claimed church membership for both parents, while nearly one-third were from homes where neither parent was a member of any church. Of these last a sizable proportion reported occasional church attendance by one or the other of their parents, though we may assume that the occasions were infrequent and the interest light. However, very few were aware of any conscious hostility toward the Church on the part of their parents—only five fathers and one mother, to be exact. The writer, visiting many of these homes, found little hostility but much confused thinking and shallow interest. It should also be stated parenthetically that the region of the study is more highly churched than many locales and that these findings would not necessarily be true of other areas. It was found to be true in the Texas study, however, as stated in the preceding chapter.

Turning from the factor of mere affiliation with a church body to the more significant factor of actual participation in the work of their respective churches, the picture looks somewhat less favorable for the parents. Only 15 per cent of the parents of these children have ever held responsible positions in their churches that their children could remember, such as singing in the choir, ushering, teaching Sunday school, treasurer, etc. Miscellaneous minor positions were reported for 5 per cent of the parents, but 80 per cent of them had never engaged in any major church activity beyond Sunday church attendance. It may be assumed that a few other parents held positions in their churches and the fact had been forgotten by the child. But it may also be assumed that if a respondent was unaware of the position held by his parent, the office or job did not exact a great amount of his time and energy.

As to church attendance by parents, the picture was considerably exaggerated in favor of the parents by their problem children. In the majority of cases there was a nostalgic yearning for the home and family situations, the intervening months having dulled the memory of their unpleasant features and enhanced the pleasant. The respondents seemed to be remembering their childhood homes and seeing the activities of their parents as they appear to the mind of a child, which tends to be generous and uncritical in its evaluation of a parent. Again, emotional immaturity, with its tendency to be less discriminating in recognizing personal or family deficiencies, is a general characteristic of juvenile delinquents.

Exaggeration notwithstanding, it is clearly true and a significant fact that a large majority of these young people came from church-connected homes, however superficial and tenuous the connections may have been. In the main they were not from homes lost to the Church. It is highly improbable that three-fifths of the fathers and four-fifths of the mothers, as was reported, attended church either regularly or occasionally (occasionally having been defined as approximately one-third of the time). On the other hand, it cannot be assumed that the fathers who never attended greatly exceed the 13 per cent reported and the mothers the 5 per cent.

In like manner, and for the reasons suggested above, these institutionally confined young people were overly generous in appraising the religious quality of their homes. Nearly three-fourths of them thought their homes were as good as the average or better. Twenty per cent thought there was some Christianity shown, but not much, while about 6 per cent rated their homes as being totally lacking in Christian influence. Having no adequate criteria by which a realistic rating could be given, the "average or better" is undoubtedly too high. But it is equally true that few of these problem children were reared in homes wherein there was no trace of Christian influence. Christianity, at least to some degree, was recognized by the vast majority of them as a factor in their homes. Secular interests and parental ego problems weakened their religious interests and the dynamic of Christian love. But these existed as embers to be rekindled and strengthened by the Church.

We should keep always in mind that there are many problem children, with serious problems of emotional and social adjustment, for every one that is charged by a court with delinquency, or committed to an institution, and with these the Church will be most effective. Serious mental or emotional defectiveness is involved in perhaps 20 per cent of the cases committed to institutions. Much of this is inherent and may require, in such cases, prolonged institutional care and/or psychiatric treatment. Many of these, however, could be rehabilitated and fitted into community life without serving a long period in an institution if the Church and family worked together as they should.

Tom was such a boy. He had spent five years in a school for mentally deficient delinquents when he was discovered by the new minister of his home church. There were no prospects of release in sight. His I.Q. marked him as a borderline moron. He was charged with a sex offense, molesting a little girl. His parents were highly respected and provided a comfortable home. The other children were completely normal and attended Sunday school frequently. The parents were members of the church but were rather inactive.

After a thorough investigation the minister was convinced that Tom's misdemeanor was not due to a serious or fixed sex deviation but that he was the victim of more intelligent boys whose teasing and suggestions had instigated the trouble. Anyway, by much persuasion and not a little pressure, Tom's release was effected. A job as messenger boy and mail distributor in a large firm was found for him. His work was satisfactory and his total adjustment good. The whole family became more active in church and community life. Tom, too, was just a kid with a problem he could not solve by himself. His mental deficiency merely made an otherwise ordinary problem more acute, more difficult for him to meet. Had he and his family been given the services that many churches are now beginning to give, he probably would not have become involved in delinquent behavior or, if so, would have been taken care of outside an institution.

The large majority of these problem children are inherently normal in their mental capacities. They are crippled emotionally by a childhood lack of love and sense of belonging or by prolonged conflict and frustration within the family relationship during later childhood. The emotional factors of immaturity, insecurity, anxiety, resentment, aggressiveness, alienation, self-absorption, etc., so frequently revealed in psychotherapy or by the Rorschach test, are the conditionings of inadequate family relationships—inadequate love, chiefly. The aggressive energies, normal to all and beneficial when rightly directed, are driven by hate and fear rather than by love. Thus they result in socially destructive relationships and behavior rather than in that which is creative and serviceable. This has been common knowledge—an accepted axiom among most psychiatrists, psychologists, and social workers. *What is not so commonly known or generally accepted is that the Church, above all other agencies, holds the key to the solution of this deficiency in family life and thus to the prevention of delinquency.* And many churches are awakening to their opportunities—are beginning to restudy, re-evaluate, and reform their role in relationship to the family.

They begin with a new look at the wedding ceremony itself. "What therefore God has joined together, let no man put asunder," whether spoken by a representative of the Church or the State, indicates that religion, and thus the Church, has a role to play in the *initiation* of the family relationship. In the vast majority of marriages these words are spoken by a clergyman in a sacred church ceremony or sacrament. The fact that most couples turn to the Church for the wedding ceremony indicates their feeling that a close relationship exists between the family and the Church, between marital adjustment and religious adjustment, but they do not know the nature and extent of that relationship. The Church is attempting to find out, and to make that relationship more effective throughout marriage.

It is well known that there is more breakdown, conflict, and divorce among couples of mixed religions than there is where both are of the same general religious background, and that there is much more among couples that take a secular attitude and apparently ignore religion or the Church altogether. Deep in their convictions and narrow in their comprehensions, husband and wife of different faiths are likely to suffer much strife and heartache. The form by which they express their faith and into which they bring their children is to them a matter not merely of life or death but of eternal bliss or damnation. Thus compromise is very difficult. Somewhat dimmed to the significance of their religious convictions by the emotional glow of their courtship and early marriage, these differences are momentarily forgotten, but they return to torture their minds when they settle down to face realistically the everyday problems of marital adjustment. It is generally recognized among leading psychologists that the greater the similarity of religious background, the greater the probability of a happy marriage; and the greater the difference, the greater is the risk of failure. The late Professor Ernest Groves devotes a whole book to the task of showing what close allies the family and the Church really are. He shows in great detail how family experiences benefit Christianity and how the Church, or minister, can help in marital adjustment. He writes:

> The family has been interpreted as inherently spiritual. It constitutes, therefore, because of its essential functions, a spiritual partner of Christianity. Its present contribution, however, is hampered by adverse influences, originating in our social environment and also as a consequence of personality defects that result in domestic maladjustments. It is obvious, therefore, that the church cannot safely look to the family to support its purposes unless at the same time it assumes the obligation to help the family function in a wholesome manner. The family has embedded in it spiritual possibilities, but these need cultivation. The family becomes for the church both obligation and opportunity. The help the church brings the family chiefly takes the form of education for family life and domestic counseling.[6]

In his address of welcome to the National Conference of Family Life, May, 1948, Lawrence H. Frank said in defining the family and its role: "It is a varying, changing, dynamic equilibrium or attempted equilibrium in which real people, real personalities, emotions, life histories, memories and expectations are engaged in trying to work out a way of life, to develop and maintain a design for living." At the national level, the Church for decades had increasingly become aware of its responsibility to the family and its opportunity to help guide the family in its search for this "way of life," this "design for living." The Church believes that the centuries have amply demonstrated that the "way of life" for the family must be found in the spirit of the Master of life who was Himself "the Way," and it believes that an adequate "design for living" can be found only in the discovery or rediscovery of God's design for the family.

Therefore the Religious Education Association maintained a department of the home from 1906 to 1920, the purpose of which was to stimulate interest in and study of family life by leaders in Christian education. The Federal Council of Churches (now National Council) set up its Committee on Marriage and the Home in 1927 and employed a full-time secretary in 1932. A big impetus was given to the movement in 1931 when the International Council of Religious Education selected "Education for Family Life" as one of four aspects of life to be given special consideration during the four ensuing years. The Joint Committee prepared the *Curriculum Guide for Work With Parents* as a guide for use by all denominations. Blanche Carrier in her *Church Education for Family Life* wrote:

> The early years of this century saw the development of a faith in education as a means of growth and hence of a graded program of instruction. By the second decade of the century a great body of materials for teaching and for leadership training had been made available, and leaders began to note that, due to a variety of causes, parents were giving decreasing time and attention to religious training in the home. But by the third decade, an increasing understanding of the child brought religious leaders back to the realization that no matter what the child's formal instruction in religion, his home life has a determinative influence on his attitudes, concepts and practices. The significance of this discovery was a large factor in the development of the current program.[7]

The denominational bodies began to face the problem in earnest during the early 1930's, although the business depression prevented the undertaking of as much new work as otherwise would have been the case. During the period of 1931 to 1935 several Protestant denominations set up committees, commissions, or departments to cope with the problem. They published bulletins and textbooks, and some of them, as constituent agencies of the International Council, developed their own programs of parent education. The larger denominations issue a monthly journal for the guidance of church school teachers. In 1934-35 the International Council made available a series of seven syndicated articles on various aspects of family life. *The Christian Home,* now one of the best known magazines for parents, began during this period as an organ of the Methodist Episcopal Church, South. In a bulletin issued by the Presbyterian Church, U.S.A. in 1934, *A Church Program for Promoting Christian Family Life,* is found this emphasis: "The point is that the

Church must not think of itself primarily in building a program for the Christian education of the family. Any plan which exploits the family for the enrichment of the Church is basically wrong. When the Church sets out to help the family, let it be for the purpose of strengthening the family 'to serve the community, the nation, and the world.'" One might add to this, to strengthen and enrich family living for its own sake.

Many leaders in the Church, along with those in secular agencies dealing with the problems of family living, recognize that much of the so-called failure and breakdown in the family is due to the rapid changes that are taking place in family organization and activity and to the higher demands the family makes of itself. These changes in function and philosophy to a more democratic, affectionate, person-centered, versatile, home-making fellowship call for more adequate preparation. The Church has taken cognizance of this and believes that a vital religion has an essential place in this preparation—that religious living and adequate family living are inseparable, that each contributes to the other and neither is the means toward which the other is the end, that spiritual values derive from family experience and that religious observances woven into family life stimulates the growth of these values. *So the Church, believing that the family asks more of itself than the secular agency or educational program can help it attain, has committed itself to an alliance with the family in an effort to work out a design for fuller living.*

The Southern Baptist Convention now publishes its magazine, *Home Life,* a magazine for better family living similar to *The Christian Home.* Nearly all of the leading denominations publish and distribute pamphlets designed to help in various aspects of family living. And one of the major emphases in their newer curriculum materials is to provide lesson units and supplementary study materials that will aid families in the attainment of a richer fellowship and expression of love—giving the children a sense of belonging and being wanted, and guiding them in the recognition of the nature and source of their frictions and in getting help for their more acute problems. Materials for each age group are geared for the attainment of adequate family living, thus building the foundations for good emotional health and social adjustment.

"I came that they may have life, and have it abundantly," said the Master of life.[8] His purpose has become the purpose of the Church that is His Body. His is the Spirit of the divine love that binds us in fellowship and enriches relationships. The Church is the body through which that *love* is most fully expressed, experienced, and mediated to others. And the abundance of life—the full, creative expression of one's highest attributes—can be attained only by the person who grows up from infancy in a home where human love enriched by divine love is freely and richly expressed. It is not the coddling love of a doting grandfather or the green, sentimental love of a moonstruck teen-ager experiencing her first grand romance. It is a love that is both generous and wise. It is a love that is firm but fair. It is a love that disciplines, molds, punishes; but it is also a love that caresses, soothes, and heals. It is a love that spurs, prods, and challenges; that encourages individuality, personal rights, and responsibilities. But it is also a love that shelters and defends, bends excess individuality to the conformity of family interests; and when conflict ensues, as it inevitably does, brings intransigent members to apologize and forgive—the generous response.

The child who grows up in such a home will not succumb to delinquency or mental illness. Foundations for responsible citizenship, effective social adjustment, and creative personal attainment will have been laid. Aggressive energies will have been brought safely under the domination of love and will never be surrendered to fear and hate. He will become a living example of the proverb, "Train up a child in the way he should go: and when he is old, he will not depart from it."[9] This truth the Church has always known but has not adequately expressed or mediated to its members. It is a truth that modern psychology and psychiatry are heralding as the great discovery of this century. It is the theme of Dr. Karl Menninger's *Man Against Himself* and *Love Against Hate* and Dr. Smiley Blanton's *Love or Perish*. The home where such love is seriously deficient will produce children with serious emotional problems, expressed outwardly in varying modes and degrees of delinquent or neurotic behavior. In a home where such love prevails even children with serious deficiencies can grow up to make a fairly satisfactory social adjustment.

It is not the purpose of this chapter to present in detail the how of this. Many have done so, for it is a widely known truth. Often in brief moments the delinquent child is aware of it. The writer held a series of talks with an attractive and intelligent 17-year-old girl who was the number one problem child of the institution where she was incarcerated. She had spent more than three years in two institutions—was too difficult to handle in the one, was released, and later was committed to the other. She was winsome at times but a perennial troublemaker, rebellious and riotous. It was in the third or fourth interview, after good rapport had been established, that she said in deep sincerity: "You know, Mr. Roberts, the only thing I've ever needed was the right kind of love." And it was an unprompted statement. No lead had been given to produce it. In almost every case the writer has worked with, love had been inadequately or unwisely expressed. Of the fifty cases studied extensively by Mrs. Holcomb, one of her conclusions was that, "Only two of the delinquents seem to have received love consistently or to an adequate degree. Over a half (56 per cent) of these boys and girls have never received any amount of love or solicitous care from their parents."[10] *The purpose of this chapter is to show that the Church is best endowed to help the family attain this quality of love relationship.* And the above outline of what the Church leaders have been doing for half a century suggests that your local church has back of it a vast amount of knowledge and materials with which to help, and that you may turn to it with confidence.

At the time of marriage most people do turn to it, for most weddings still occur in a church or are solemnized by a minister. Persons who ask the Church to unite them in marriage should give the Church the opportunity, when help is needed, to keep the marriage solvent and successful. The couple are given a better start when married by a minister, and at the altar of a church. The impression is more or less deeply made that God is in the union and has an essential part in uniting them. A Christian interpretation of love and marriage is given. God is love, and love is of the soul—not merely a physical attraction or emotional response. Mature love is shown to be spiritual in essence. The New Testament concept of love as *agape* is interpreted in its relationship to love as *eros*—that as the two become one it is not only body cleaving to body but mind to mind and soul to soul. They are shown that in their wedded love is the wedding of agape and eros—that their sexual union to be richly satisfying must have in it a deeply spiritual content. As such the sexual or genital expression of love becomes exclusive, a one-man-one-woman relationship for life. The sexual union becomes a sacrament of love, where each gives of himself to the full—body, mind, and soul—and seeks the other's fullest enrichment, not merely his own physical gratification.

Christian marriage is interpreted to them as a sacred obligation, a covenant and commitment—not merely a personal contract to be broken when either is dissatisfied with his bargain. It is a commitment of each to the other and a covenant between them and their God. It is a pledge to stick it out "for better or worse"—no, to work it out through better and worse, and to give the Church a chance to help them work it out. It is a pledge to love, honor, and cherish with a mature love that is patient, long-suffering, and strong —a love that gives and seeks to heal, rather than an immature, demanding love. It recognizes that God is in their marriage as long as love is kept at a spiritual level, that it cannot be broken off without His consent, and that He is available and able to help them work through their difficulties. They, the marrying couple, are helped to see that human personality is adjustable when faith and love rule over fear and hate and that a redeeming, divine Love is available to help in the adjustment and to enrich the relationship.

Furthermore, the wedding partners are shown that to maintain a healthful spiritual life is the most essential factor in the development of a rich and permanent love relationship. As physical health and attractiveness are essential to the erotic satisfactions of their love, spiritual vitality is essential to the soul phase of their union. And if they permit the life of the soul, their spiritual health, to deteriorate and die, love will die at its deeper level. If it survives at all it will be thin, a skimmed milk sort of thing, unnourishing and unfulfilling. Eros and agape will have become divorced. God will have departed from their union. To maintain spiritual health and vigor, worship is essential, for worship is spiritual calisthenics. Through worship the deeper soul responses are made, the deeper level of personality expressed, the rich capacities for a life of faith and love developed. Through worship the soul is made sensitive and responsive and the channels are opened to the reception of a divine, enriching love. Through worship the covenanted individuals become aware of divine forgiveness and acceptance, are given a sense of eternal security and eternal love, and are thus able to surrender their fears, hates, and defenses and to think of themselves and each other as they ought. By the concept of marriage it conveys and the worship aids it provides, the Church is the agency that can help the family attain and maintain the rich atmosphere of love and trust that ought to prevail in the home.

Many churches sponsor clinics or classes for young expectant mothers and place the best available literature into their hands. Then when the expected and wanted child is born and presented at the altar for baptism or dedication, the church covenants with the parents to give its every aid—to unite its forces with those of the home, that the child may grow "in wisdom and stature, and in favour with God and man"; that it may have life abundantly, to the fullness of its capacities.[11] Again, the church places into the hands of the parents the best available literature on child care and development. Short courses are given by the church, often in co-operation with other community agencies, on husband-wife relations and child-parent relations. Children are taken into the church school at an early age and guided in their growing experiences to respond to life with faith and love. More—and better—our churches are learning to gear their religious teaching to the natural insights and emotional responses of the child, so that life becomes and remains a sacred adventure for the individual, with his religion a dynamic force within the soul, not merely a concept of the mind. More and more churches are directing their Christian training emphasis to the home in a home-and-church-together type of training program. The church school provides the lecture phase (storytelling and Bible reading), and as the child grows older the school and community become laboratories for experimenting in love and faith. Thus family (and community) experiences provide class materials for learning discussions and class experiences, and insights are carried into the home (and community) to enrich life there. Too, the churches are providing evening activities and sponsoring camps where the whole family participates in fun and fellowship. They encourage families to spend more time together in work and worship and play, thus enriching family love and fellowship. And when the children reach the turbulent teen age, their churches are still with them, providing in their camps and Sunday schools lesson units on self-understanding, family relations, social ethics and relationships, boy-girl relationships and preparation for marriage. Dr. Blanton, in his *Love or Perish*, writes:

> Every child compels its parents to go through the whole history of civilization all over again. Just as the human embryo recapitulates the story of evolution, so the child repeats in rapid succession the many stages of development that carried men from primitive savagery to contemporary culture. The parent must accompany the child on this difficult journey, acting as chief interpreter and guide. He must give the directions at each turn of the trail, and it will be largely due to his skill if the child emerges finally as a loving and balanced human being.
>
> If many parents, despite their best efforts, fail to achieve this ultimate goal with their children, it is usually because they misconceive a central aspect of their role. Most of us understand fully the part we must play as good providers for our children. We readily comprehend the measures that must be taken to protect them from danger, to fill their nutritional needs, and to assure their physical health and development as they move along the path to maturity.
>
> What throws most parents into confusion and bewilderment is the basic problem of curbing the child's primitive impulses. Each new member of the human race brings with him all the ancient threats and fears that mankind has struggled so long

to subdue. In every child's unconscious mind lie the crawling beasts of selfish aggression, of murderous hate, and of powerful sexual drives that will run rampant if not controlled.

The parent is the delegate appointed by civilization to tame these destructive forces. It is a mighty responsibility—yet most of us are given precious little equipment with which to carry it out! Our instruction book usually contains little but our past fears and our own faltering solutions as the models to follow. If we look at human history for our cue, we see that the emphasis has almost invariably been focused on the technique of suppression rather than of enlightened guidance. Mankind, faced with its own stubbornness and recalcitrance, has always found it easier to take the role of a stern policeman than of a loving teacher.[12]

More than any other institution or agency, the Church is endowed, and many churches are prepared, to help the faltering parent with the responsibility and opportunity that God and society have thrust upon him. The frightened or irresponsible parent cannot delegate this authority to his church, *but his church is the one supporting agency that can walk with him every step of the way from the birth of the child to its maturity and can aid most effectively in the guiding process.* For it provides not only the best in literature aids and insights, but it mediates into the home a quality of divine love that will compensate for a multitude of mistakes in technique. In an atmosphere of Christian faith and love, and with the full support of his alerted church, no parent need fear this responsibility.

First Community Church of Columbus, Ohio, was selected by *The Christian Century* as one of the twelve greatest churches in America. Its outstanding ministry to all aspects of family life—a ministry that is virtually "from the cradle to the grave"—is a major factor in its greatness. In a pamphlet entitled *I Am the First Community Church* its various activities and services are described. Following are a few excerpts:

Believing that each child should be conceived and born in a love that is of God, we see that every resource is given to guiding the right two people to marry, helping them both to realize that only as they love God can their own love find permanent fulfillment; that only as they seek to do His will as a primary purpose in life can they know together a companionship that stimulates the God in each and that links them in union with the God in each other.

It is our purpose that each child be so loved that he in turn learns to love, growing above the cradle stage of self love to the place where the love of God flows through him out to other people. We seek to instill in parents the wisdom that gives to each child the discipline of earned recognition, a sense of such belonging that he is at home in his world, a feeling of such security that he may be free to live by some law within himself rather than be a victim of outer pressures.

Within the planned activities in the church building, in each family circle, in each schoolroom, on the playground, we seek to help each child, first of all, grow in the spirit and way of Christ. Second, build fellowship and friendship in the spirit of Jesus. Third, learn the fullest meaning and skill of work, so as to be able to make the best contribution to the human family while he earns his own bread in love. Fourth, become big enough for sacramental marriage. Fifth, grow through worship and prayer into an increasing awareness of God, so that the life he lives is the very life of God. Sixth, find the resources of the Bible, of music, of art, of beauty, of all the gifts of the sciences for the fullest growth of the spiritual life. And seventh, make his best gift, by his voice, his vote, and his leadership to building the beloved community locally, nationally and over the world.

Believing that the family is the major school of Christian living, we try to encourage each family to be the church every day, in all its relationships. We visit each new mother, taking a rose to her and sharing with her a high inspiration and vision for her child. Young children are brought into the sanctuary to be consecrated to the Lord, and parents pledge themselves to bring their children up in the nurture and admonition of the Lord. We visit in their homes. We invite them to meet together to study how their vows may be faithfully fulfilled; study groups in all phases of guidance and leadership of children are provided for parents. Clinic sessions are held where help may be secured for special problem situations; we work with the school in the interest of special problem cases. We seek to work closely with the chief of police, the courts, all the social agencies. It is our purpose to hallow all their efforts.[13]

After a description of the multiple and varied activities and services for every age group, the personal ministry of the church is described:

We seek to make every resource available for the guidance of Christian growth from the time of conception. When it is discovered that a child is having difficulty or is not making normal progress in his growth, we try to get all the adults who are sharing with him or her together. This includes the parents, the school and church leaders, the physician, and in very serious cases, the psychiatrist. If the child gets into difficulty with the law, then the chief of police joins in the conference. The purpose is not to rally against the child, but to bring all the understanding possible among those who live and share with him. If all of his adult friends have enough understanding, the solution of his problems becomes much easier.

There are many personal interviews with parents, with children and also with their teachers. Sometimes if a child has an opportunity to talk with an understanding friend outside his home and even outside the classroom, it adds to his security and sustaining.

. . . . . .

Our church feels that it is important to have a program of marriage education throughout the various ages. Young people should be helped to understand the home as an institution; they should see it as a part of God's plan. They need help in finding the greatest fulfillment with their present homes; there should be constant emphasis that will help them come to an understanding of dating from a Christian point of view, and to grow in a Christian rather than a Hollywood interpretation of love.[14]

Books are mentioned that are given to young people to guide their thinking on courtship and marriage, then:

Before a couple is married in our church, they come to the ministers for counseling. One of the steps in this process is for them both to fill out the Bernreuter Personality Schedule. They are given one of these blanks with lines showing the personality relationship; they can see what the potentialities are for finding companionship. . . . The pre-marital counseling includes the following types of studies: Are you really in love? Are you emotionally ready for marriage? Can you find a companionship that will grow with the years? Have you faced the adjustments of marriage? What part is God to have in your home? Understanding and appreciating the ways by which love may ever grow and become increasingly spiritual.

In addition to this, there is a thorough study of the ceremony and the meaning of the vows. There is help in laying the foundation for the family budget, including planning for children.[15]

The reader may well see why Community Church of Columbus is a great church, and why so few of its children would become serious problem children, reverting to either delinquency or mental illness. Few churches are at present providing services so complete and of such high quality as does this great institution. But under the guidance of their denominational boards and commissions, more and more local churches are approximating more and more closely the above-described family services. Some day these services will be the norm for the local church. Then delinquency will be a rare phenomenon among the families of the Church and mental illness greatly reduced. The local churches hold the key to enriched family living and thus to the prevention of delinquency.

While a large majority of the delinquent children and their parents studied by the writer had some connection with a church, notably lacking were the special church-sponsored services and activities for children and families such as those described above. Church for most of them consisted entirely of the formal Sunday school class and morning worship. As was previously suggested, the sermons and teaching were not well geared to the growing problems and interests of the children. A small minority of these problem children attended some sort of evening program for children and youth such as Junior League or Christian Endeavor. But questioning during personal interviews revealed that in most instances these were little more than an extension of the Sunday school class type of religious instruction. Of the thirty cases studied intensively by the writer, not one had been interviewed by his pastor before becoming involved in the delinquent behavior that resulted in committal. And in no case was the youth aware of any specific family service activities sponsored by their churches with the exception of a few Sunday school picnics and the annual Children's Day program. Undoubtedly a few of the churches were doing something more for their families, but it had not come to the attention or aid of these problem children.

These children suffered the consequences of their churches' failure to live up to their potentialities. Most churches are resolved that this failure will not long continue, and they are rapidly implementing their good resolutions with increasingly effectual programs. Whether residing in your home or your community, the problem child is your problem. And whether or not you are a member of it, the local church in your community is your church and for your service. It can help your problem children and families find the solution to their problems.

6.

The Redeeming Fellowship

CENTRAL IN THE PROBLEM OF THE PROBLEM CHILD is the matter of adjustment to other persons. If the child fails to develop satisfying relationships with those who mean most to him, he will tend to develop patterns of exaggerated dependency, aggressiveness, or withdrawal—sometimes alternating between two of these. Karen Horney, widely read psychiatrist, has developed this thesis; and it has become generally accepted. She describes these states as moving toward people, moving against people, and moving away from people. If these patterns continue to develop, without remedial help, the end result is delinquency or mental illness. Whether or not these end results accrue, problem behavior and unhappiness prevail under such conditions. Fellowship is inadequate, and with it is the inadequacy to express love and to form worthy friendships. The Rorschach tests repeatedly show this to be one of the outstanding traits of delinquent children. To help build satisfying friendships and adequate interpersonal relationships based on brotherly love is a primary function of the Church.

In a previous publication the present writer develops the basic need for social fellowship as follows:

> The baby at birth stands at the threshold of becoming a human being. During his embryonic development he goes through several stages that roughly resemble the evolutionary development of animal life. At birth he steps out into a world of human relations. He has only a few specific and adaptive

forms of behavior—breathing, sucking, and eliminating—just that which is essential for the maintenance of organic life. The rest of him is a squirming mass of unorganized, unco-ordinated activity. He is human in potentiality only (unlimited potentiality). He must become both human and divine. Personality must be attained. It is a process of becoming. The child must learn to walk and to talk like people. He must learn to think and to appreciate and to love like a human. He must develop the traits of character and personality that make of him a true person. To do this he must live with his fellow man and share deeply in many and varied human relationships. . . .

The child who is reared in a normal family will develop all the essential traits of human living and adjustment even though he is cut off from all other social contacts and relations. . . . But to develop richness, fullness, and balance of personality the child must engage in an ever-widening circle of social contacts and relationships with many and varied types of personalities. Most neurotic and delinquent patterns of behavior result from, or are symptoms of, faulty social adjustments, largely due to faults within the family. But even as wholesome social adjustment depends on wholesome family living, the family as a healthful nursery of humanity depends on wide social contacts. Were there no contacts beyond the immediate family, human personality would turn in upon itself and die in the quagmire of incest. The fear and horror of incest as revealed in ancient mythology shows that primitive man sensed this, though his knowledge of human personality and the requirements of its development was all but void. And only as social contacts become wide and varied can the most suitable mating be attained—young man and young woman finding one another with mutual capacities for sharing richly and fully. The way of life is a way of social fellowship.

A mature and adequately expressed parental love is an absolute necessity in laying the emotional foundations for wholesome character and personality growth. But more than that is needed. The growing person must experience and respond to the love of humanity—humanity as it is experienced one by one in an ever-widening circle of fellowship. Mother humanity must take the place of one's organic mother as the provider of a mature sense of security and the many personal satisfactions. Each person is largely a product of two family lines that merged in the marriage of his parents. But each individual child has potentialities that, in order to develop and satisfy, call for more than the family fellowship can provide. Shared experiences in varying degrees of depth with a large variety of persons are necessary to develop a full and well-balanced personality and the capacity for a rich and mature love for one's own family and for mankind.[1]

That the problem of forming adequate teen-age friendships and love responses is fraught with difficulty goes without argument. It is the perennial problem of parents and youth counselors. It is a bigger and more vital problem for the kids themselves. Having dates and fun on these dates, becoming popular with their peers, especially with those of the opposite sex, growing in their capacity to express and experience love, all adds up to a very complex problem and a very important one. Those who fail to solve this problem satisfactorily usually are our problem children. Behavior extremes develop—extremes of withdrawal, dependency, or aggressiveness. These young people need a multiple variety of shared experiences with many persons of both sexes in a wide field of social fellowship to complete their development. They need to be bound together in fellowship and mutual affection, sharing together in a variety of activities and events. But how can affection be shared adequately by teen-agers without becoming involved in too free an expression of sex? The problem child has a serious problem at this point. If it isn't solved he often becomes a problem adult. The too-free expression of sex is notable among delinquents, a common form of delinquency; and extreme suppression of sex ranks high among the causative factors or symptoms of neurotic behavior.

The local church that is normative holds the key to the solution of these problems. It is in essence a true fellowship. The first-century Christians aspired to, and in a fair measure attained, a quality of fellowship characterized by their Master in His relations with His intimate friends. In small groups they mingled freely in a true fellowship of worship, of service, of social intercourse. Potluck

suppers, the common meal, were frequent. There was much sharing—mentally, spiritually, socially, and materially. Friendship was
the prevailing atmosphere; love was the bond. It was love experienced as agape (spiritual love, God as Love), and not as eros.
The two may have gotten mixed at times, for these early Christians
were not perfect. This motivating and binding love in the fellowship made of the Church an enlarged family. God was experienced
as perfect parental love, and the members loved one another as
brothers and sisters. *Thus the Church then was, and now often is,
the larger family that forms an essential link between the individual
family unit and society at large, aiding in the maturing and social-
izing process.* Too, in instances where the individual family unit
fails as a fellowship unit based on love, the Church can in a large
measure compensate for that failure. Within the fold of the Church,
and in the smaller, more intimate fellowships that compose the
total congregation, the child or youth is led to experience the
warmth of human love and friendship that carries an overtone of
divine love. In this atmosphere he learns to experience forgiveness
in both directions. He learns to accept himself in spite of his inadequacies, and his family in spite of their failures, because God and
children of God have accepted him as a child of God. In this
atmosphere he can learn, though delayed, to love himself adequately
and thus to love others adequately. He can then express love and
his growing love capacities in wise and wholesome relationships.
Under the guiding experience of divine love, his sexual emotions
can be more easily sublimated or diffused into warm affectional
relationships free of gross lust and compulsive sex drives. In the
chapter on fellowship as an essential way of life cited above, the
writer continues:

> These early Christians had a name for it, Koinonia. For in
> this fellowship they were not only conscious of self and others
> in deep empathetic oneness; they were conscious of Christ. He
> was in the fellowship. He was the Spirit that bound them
> together into the organic whole. As the chemical compound has
> characteristics other than its constituent elements, organic wholes
> possess qualities over and above that of the individual con-

stituents. The individual who loses himself in the fellowship (grafted into the organic body) finds himself at a heightened sense of selfhood. He attains true self-awareness and greater freedom to be. Thus redemption is carried on within the fellowship that is the body of Christ or an organ in that body. The qualities of the whole become characteristic of the individual who has been compounded into the whole. The deeper meanings of life are conveyed to the minds of each (within limitations) as they merge in a oneness of experience. Thus there is true communion at the deeper levels of being, providing the basis for true community living, necessary for effective society. It is a communication that is carried on with or without the structural form of speech and the structural imagery that words convey. It is a communication of mind and spirit, structural and nonstructural, the heights and depths of experience, of meaning —the fullest self-awareness, other-awareness, and God-awareness. Christ as Truth and Love is in the fellowship and is experienced most fully therein. But it is a fellowship, not just a social gathering of individuals.

Christ is the Head, the Mind, the Soul of the Church, which is His Body—the institutional and eternal Body that He created and in which He abides. It is the continuum of revelation and redemption. In it is awareness of the way of life and the spiritual dynamic to follow that way. The Church is a Fellowship and must provide for fellowship. In the larger local church the total congregation is too large for the newly inducted member to find fellowship. It must be composed of many small fellowships —small groups of similar ages or interests or needs. In the small, more nearly homogeneous group—joined together in song, in prayer, in special service projects, in the common meal, in simple conversation, and in a variety of social activities—fellowship becomes a reality. Established in the small group it carries over into the larger and becomes the cement of society. It is the way of life.[2]

Paul severely criticized the church at Corinth because of its failure to maintain a true fellowship. In the first place the congregation was split into segments by their personal tastes and human loyalties and prejudices. Some favored Peter, others Apollos, and still others held to Paul. In this spirit of division they lost contact with Christ and the binding force of divine love was broken. Then, secondly, when they came together in the supposed fellowship of the common meal (potluck), after which they observed the sacrament of Holy Communion, they divided into separate "cliques" based on social and economic class distinction. "But in the following instructions I do not commend you, because when you come together it is not for the better but for the worse. For, in the first place, when you assemble as a church, I hear that there are divisions among you; and I partly believe it, for there must be factions among you in order that those who are genuine among you may be recognized. When you meet together, it is not the Lord's supper that you eat. For in eating, each one goes ahead with his own meal, and one is hungry and another is drunk. What! Do you not have houses to eat and drink in? Or do you despise the church of God and humiliate those who have nothing? What shall I say to you? Shall I commend you in this? No, I will not." (1 Corinthians 11:17-22, r.s.v.)

One of the most common criticisms made of their respective churches by delinquents with whom the writer has talked was that the church people were not friendly. We who have been active in the work of the church know also that many others use this as an excuse for not attending or joining a church. And we know that in many instances the criticism is unwarranted—that it is the critical person who has alienated himself from friendly church people or who is merely using it as a convenient alibi. However, there is enough truth in the accusation to make it stick. The writer has felt the coolness and lack of true fellowship in more than one church and is reminded of one particular church composed chiefly of middle-aged and older persons (and of middle class) who actually seemed to resent young people being in the church. These rowdy youth, they felt, were not pious but noisy and boisterous and desecrated the "house of God." To them the church building had become a sacred relic more precious than human personality. They had lost sight of the Church as a redeeming fellowship. And notable among the churches from which most of the delinquent children studied by the writer came was the deficiency of fellowship activities for children and youth. Personal counseling to help the problem child fit himself into the program was generally lacking. This is usually needed, for the problem child has grown barriers within himself that makes fellowship difficult. But this is the subject of the next chapter.

The fellowship ideal based on "brotherly affection one for the other" has again caught hold of the churches, perhaps as never before since the first century. The pulpit, focal point of a prophetic Church that receives and proclaims the eternal Word, and the altar, focal point of a sacramental Church that recognizes and responds to the divine Presence, are still of primary significance and emphasis—one church placing a little more stress on the one and another on the other. But the significance of these are coming more and more to be seen as the foci of the elliptical body, the fellowship. Their values, while primary, are nevertheless instrumental rather than terminal. The value lies in that they are the foci around which is proscribed the body of divine-human fellowship. All activity and all emphasis terminate in the fellowship, the koinonia in which the divine is experienced with the human, in which agape purifies and redeems eros. Thus the Church to an ever-increasing degree is becoming the larger family, the smaller and more specialized community, that receives without merit the divine love of God as eternal and infinite Parent and expresses its own divinely enriched human love to brother and sister humanity, especially within its own family, wherein "there is neither Jew nor Greek . . . bond nor free . . . male nor female." (Galatians 3:28, K.J.V.) This is a fellowship wherein a divinely enriched, sex-sublimated, diffused, and truly brotherly affection can be richly and freely expressed. It is now being seen as the goal toward which the churches are bending their efforts, the norm for the true Church, the goal of its high calling, toward which it is now pressing forward, confessing and forgetting its past failures in its renewed commitment to this end.

The problem child, whether his symptoms point toward delinquency or mental illness, is not redeemed by listening to the proclaimed word which he has rationally accepted nor by a punctilious observance of the ritual which he may perform conscientiously. He, by the very nature of his problem, has a sense of alienation from

God and man, a lack of worth. Not having experienced love adequately during childhood, he developed the more or less unconscious conviction that somehow he was not of sufficient worth to merit love. Whether he moves toward, against, or away from people in patterns of dependency, aggressiveness, or withdrawal, and whether he accepts rationally the body of beliefs of his church, the inner citadel of his life, his deeper selfhood, remains unchanged. But when he is grafted into the body of the Church and becomes a part of the fellowship, the atmosphere or life or spirit of the fellowship slowly permeates his inner being and he begins to experience forgiveness, acceptance, the love of God, and friendship of man without relationship to his own sense of worth. He gains a new perspective of himself and others. The relative insignificance of the value differences or merit differences among his fellow men is felt more clearly as he experiences the love of and acceptance by the absolute Person. Thus a new and true sense of humanity is attained. He can drop his ego defenses, forgive and accept forgiveness, love his fellow man and receive his love, now feeling himself to be of equal worth to all men but without merit before God. He has learned, too, in the crucible of divine-human fellowship, that love is not determined by worth or merit, that his old fears and defenses were groundless; and he becomes freed of his compulsions and fears—freed to love and to adjust mentally and socially. He becomes the redeemed within the fellowship.

So the Church is finally coming into its own as the divine-human fellowship—imperfect but groping and growing, failing and finding. The Universal Church is composed of its smaller fellowships or denominations. The local church is composed of numerous smaller homogeneous fellowships. The road to universal brotherhood, to world-wide fellowship, is one of stages—the individual family, the fellowship within the fellowship, then the fullness of spiritual maturity when God is truly Father and all humanity is Mother and all people are brothers and sisters in the universal family of God. To attain this is to experience the fullness of security and the oneness of fullest acceptance, the fullest freedom, and the ability to live by love and faith. *In being such an institution the Church plays a dis-*

tinctive and unique role in the redemption or rehabilitation of the problem person.

The Church is becoming self-conscious of its role and is approaching it with humility and faith. The formerly designated "Christian Endeavor" and "Epworth League" and "Baptist Young People's Union" have become Youth Fellowships. Programs and facilities are provided to bring young people together in a variety of shared experiences—in a fellowship of worship, of service, of recreation and social living. Describing the local youth program, George A. Warmer, Jr., the minister of the Holliston Avenue Methodist Church of Pasadena, California, writes:

> Our whole youth lounge program, which is helping us expand our approach to youth, is a special interest approach to our community needs. Here on every weekday noon and evening, except Monday, we open a spacious, commodious lounge and basement playrooms for the use of our young people. This is their "home away from home." Modern life is lived at such a pace that our own young people are spending less and less time at home and more and more time in places which tend to undermine the home. Instead of saying, "You must not go with that bad crowd, or enter that tavern or road house," we are endeavoring to take the more positive approach by furnishing a modern community center for youth. A host or hostess is always present when the lounge is open and every care is taken to help our young people study, play, eat, have music, or just grow up in a friendly atmosphere pervaded by Jesus' spirit.[3]

Lesson units for group discussion are built around the experiences, problems, and needs of young people as recognized by themselves. They select the units of study that appeal to their own interests and needs. In an informal setting a true fellowship of shared ideas and experiences develops. With minds alive to issues and problems of their own time and age, and to their own personal and inter-personal relationships, they turn from discussion to the altar. In a group worship experience, their problems and differences and group convictions are directed Godward. Differences are forgotten as they unite with one another, and with the Church of the ages, in prayer and in a deep affirmation of faith and love. Then they go out to serve their church or community in projects of service. Fellowship teams go out to help other churches develop youth activities. Teams help with the church nursery, help with the church grounds, raise money for special projects, work in community centers and social service agencies, or in any of a hundred and one things that need doing. Working in groups in a true fellowship of service, these young people learn one of the great secrets of good living—how to have fun doing good. Having fun working together in that which is truly service makes for true fellowship, and it is a fellowship in which He who "came not to be ministered unto but to minister" becomes known to them as a co-worker. Add to all this the camping program sponsored by churches, and available to most of their youth and older children, and we have the beginnings of fellowship at its best. One of our great churches describes the value of its camping program, which is typical, in the following terms:

> Here they come to experience as nearly as may be possible any place, the Kingdom of God. A fellowship grows in which the best is called out of each and each makes his best contribution to all. Barriers disappear and love flows through the fellowship, giving each person his place and each person a purpose. In the camp there is play, work, planning, worship, singing, study, and truth-seeking. The day is started with personal prayer and concluded with cabin devotions. There are Vesper Services, great fun sessions, and forums. They build Christian lives, train Christian leaders, and hallow all life.[4]

A fellowship project of great redemptive value was carried out by this same church. It, too, is being duplicated by many, with many variations. This is the story:

> We had a group of boys with whom both the church and school were having a great deal of trouble. The Cub Scouts had lost control of them completely. We employed a young man from the university part time, who organized them into a club. They met weekly. At times they had joint meetings with their fathers. They learned to do things as a group. In time they have become a very fine Church School class and the school leaders have been

amazed with the change. Sometimes the boys of greatest possi-
bility are the fullest of tricks and most mischievous. To put
them out of the class is not a solution.[5]

To put the problem child out of the church or the school or the
community is not a solution, nor is it necessary except in a relatively
small number of defective cases. *The solution is to build around him
a redeeming fellowship.* In the above instance a group of problem
children well on their way to delinquency found the solution to their
problems in a fellowship which their church, better than any other
agency, could provide.

Whether the symptomatic behavior of the problem child turns
toward delinquency or mental illness, a basic factor in his problem
is the element of faith. And faith is very largely a product of fellowship. It was shown in a previous chapter that the delinquent child
usually believes in God, the Church, and the Bible. The problem is
one of the depth or degree of faith. His faith was adequate for fair
weather but not for the tempest. Perhaps his faith is as great as that
of many normal young persons whose more sheltered lives kept them
out of the tempests. Like that of most persons, the faith of the
delinquent and neurotic is immature and inadequate, unable to hold
him steadfast in the crisis. His faith is largely assent of the mind
and not the deeper "heart" conviction. He depends too much upon
himself, others having failed him too often, and when self fails
his faith in self and in God wavers. He feels insecure, uncertain,
alienated from God and man. Again and again these problem children would testify, "Mostly I believe in God, but when things go
wrong I have doubts." They have not developed the quality of faith
described by Paul, "My grace is sufficient for you, for my power is
made perfect in weakness." (2 Corinthians 12:9, R.S.V.) A sense of
personal alliance with the Almighty is not theirs in their time of
need. Religious faith has not attained maturity until it can hold to,
or holds the person by, trust in God regardless of circumstances.
It is the Church's responsibility and opportunity to help the problem
child develop such mature faith. No other institution can do it, and
there is no solution to his problem until it is done. It is attained
in the fellowship.

Faith in God and faith in others are closely correlated. Faith in God gives a sense of divine acceptance, a greater sense of worth and self-acceptance, and an opening of the way to a fuller sense of social acceptance. But the problem child has failed to establish adequate relationships with those who count most in his early life. He has felt rejected and has reacted by moving against (in rebellion) or toward (in abject dependency) or away from (in neurotic flight) his fellow man. The foundations of faith in God, in himself, and in his fellow man are shaky. If he is received into the Christian fellowship, is accepted by its members and loved by them and learns to trust them, his faith in self and God will grow into true self-acceptance and a true sense of divine acceptance. He must grow his own faith. No one can give him a ready-made faith. But in the atmosphere of faith and love generated by the Christian fellowship his faith will grow. And as he accepts the fellowship he accepts that which makes it distinctive—its faith and love.

This will be no easy task for the fellowship. It will provide the supreme Christian test. But in this it will be good for the fellowship as well as for the problem child it is trying to redeem. Often it means to love the enemy, for the rebellious delinquent has become the enemy of the true fellowship. More often it means to love the unlovable, the suspicious, the exasperating. It means to seek out these problem persons with patience and sympathy, based on true understanding rather than on maudlin sentimentality, and to cultivate their confidence and friendship though rejected again and again. It means a literal and realistic obedience to the Master's command to go out into the highways and byways and bring them in. It is evangelism in depth. Only the Church carries this commission. Only the Church is promised the agape, the divine love which alone is sufficient dynamic to do the job.

In every church there is someone who has overcome mountainous obstacles by faith and to the enrichment of his faith. He may have been an alcoholic or mentally ill, or he may have been delinquent in earlier years. These persons can be the key members of the fellowship, acting as the catalytic agent that induces the necessary response on the part of the problem personality and leading to his transformation and spiritual union with the fellowship. Those who have gone through tribulation, who have faced great temptation and have fallen but again climbed to the heights, are they who can best kindle hope and initiate faith in one who is still down. The Church can best use these special servants in its various special fellowships. It is becoming alert to the opportunity.

Delinquent and neurotic patterns are not limited to the poverty-stricken, but cover the gamut of economic classes. Nevertheless, poverty is a factor in delinquency and there are more problem children among the economically handicapped than among families of comfortable means. The family that is constantly on, or frequently on and off, public assistance is confronted with more than an economic problem. With more or less justification parents and children feel that they are alienated from "better" people. The lack of money, clothes, and a suitable home prevent much social intercourse. Even in the church they feel slighted or ill at ease, "haven't proper clothes"; and so they shun the fellowship. Unable to buy the things or do the things other children take for granted, because they lack money and social opportunity, the children are confronted with a serious problem and real temptation. Fellowship is essential, so they find it within the street gang or they create it by whatever means and in whatever mode circumstances permit. The Church as a fellowship of love is now beginning to see its opportunity and is going out to win various members of such families into its various fellowships. Sometimes provision is made for them to obtain clothing free or at a nominal cost in a face-saving manner. They are enlisted in service activities side by side with their more fortunate neighbors and accepted as co-workers in a worthwhile service, giving to them a sense of worth. The process of redemption proceeds from there.

Always the mentally retarded is a problem child, because it is more difficult for him to solve the problems of adjustment in a complex society. The large majority of delinquent children have normal intelligence and average only a little lower than their nondelinquent peers. But a much larger percentage of mentally retarded children get into trouble than do their mentally superior peers, simply because the complex problems of adjustment are more often too difficult for them. If, however, they are given additional help, with understanding and love, they need not become involved in delinquent behavior, and probably will not. To provide this additional help, with love and understanding, is the job of the Church. The youth fellowship adequately coached can find a place for these retarded, though not too seriously deficient, youngsters. And there are social and service activities in which they can participate effectively. Furthermore, the larger church can, as some are doing, provide a special class with trained teachers for these mentally handicapped children. Four or five of them are as many as one teacher can handle. Several smaller churches can co-operate to provide this special service. Taking care of themselves personally and growing socially and morally are the emphases given. The Church whose God is Love must provide a fellowship of love for all, even the mentally handicapped. It is beginning to do this job which no other institution can do as well. It can bridge the gap between the special fellowship it provides and normal society.

Finally we come to those persons who have been overwhelmed by their problems. They could not relate themselves adequately to the people who mattered most in their lives. Aggressive rebellion born of frustration kept them striking out at society until society in self-protection committed them to an institution for delinquents. Or else they alienated themselves from a baffling society by flight from reality and were committed to a hospital for the mentally ill. Institutional care with highly specialized professional service may for a time be necessary. But even here a fellowship of love and faith, and frequent association with normal people who care, provide the real cure. So again it is the Church who carries its fellowship to these unfortunate victims of a baffling society. Their illness, social or mental, was caused by their alienation from people. How, then, can they be redeemed by shutting them away from normal society? During this period of confinement a bridge must be built that links them with a small but meaningful society. The suspension cables of that bridge are faith and love.

To help these, a church sends its group of selected visitors to the mental hospital. By showing a friendly interest and confidence in the patients these visitors slowly induce them to participate in fellowship activities—worship, recreation, and carefully chosen service projects, sewing and other handwork for the needy. These visiting fellowships do not merely "put on" worship services or dramatic productions for the patients. They win their confidence and induce them to become participants in a fellowship of worship and recreation. If their faith is real and their love is true—and it must be to help, for you can't fool the mentally ill with a superficial concern—slowly the patient will come out of his protective shell, accept the members of the fellowship and its spirit, begin to trust himself and others, and finally attain an adequate linkage with society and with God. It is slow, and not always complete. But it is working, as many churches are proving.

Similar fellowship activities are being developed by church groups for inmates of schools for delinquents. While temporary restriction may be necessary in many cases, as suggested above, the cure lies in developing or redeveloping capacities for adjustment to normal society. Barriers of alienation must be broken down, which cannot be done behind rigid walls of institutional confinement. Youth fellowships from neighborhood churches with true understanding and concern can bridge this psychological and institutional "moat" with a variety of social, recreational, and other fellowship activities. A ball game between the church and institution team may be followed by a mixer party or square dance. Joint participation in worship activities and dramatics has rewarding effects. Selected groups from an institution may be taken to a nearby Youth Fellowship religious and social event, or to a church camp for a week. This type of remedial service is just beginning, but its possibilities are immense. Understanding, acceptance, trust, and love by a small group of normal, wholesome people provides the best cure for both the delinquent and the mentally ill. This is a primary function of the Church. In carrying out this function it has no equal, for it does not work alone. A divine love and acceptance may be experienced through such fellowship that includes prayer.

Jesus prayed regularly and especially in emergency situations. Results were phenomenal. And man has always prayed in times of crisis, sensing that his own powers are inadequate and that somehow divine resources are available, and believing that "Man's extremity is God's opportunity." Our problem children in most cases are not nearly so hopeless as we fear. Perhaps that is one of the main reasons why we have not turned more fully to God for help, but have still hoped to find the solution by man's wisdom and technique alone. There are other reasons, however. Devout Christians for centuries have prayed for the solution of these same problems, and for one success they have seen a hundred failures. Too, they have seen what appeared to be miraculous cures by so-called "faith healers," but in connection with this, they have seen so many pseudo-cures and so much ignorance, superstition, and unwholesome emotionalism that the whole thing became discredited in the eyes of most sensitive and sensible people, and they, shall we say, threw out the baby with the dirty bath water. Again, churchman and nonchurchman alike, we all became so enamored with the marvelous achievements of "science" during the past century that we glossed over the divine promises in an effort to make eternal Truth conform to the observations and findings of natural science.

Thus the element of the miraculous and the realization of a divine power or love that heals man's physical, mental, and social diseases became largely lost, even to the people of the Church—to those who supposedly are the children of faith. Some of the smaller religious sects, though still clouded with elements of unreality and extremism, have rendered a very great service to mankind by reminding the Church of its neglect and calling it back to its opportunity—to the divine promises and the power that is available and able to fulfill them. Now the churches are awake and have come to realize that the Christ of miraculous healing who made those promises to the Church is a real and vital force in the fellowship and is available to do the mighty works He did then. It has come to realize that the Christian fellowship reaches its apex in the fellowship of prayer, where two or three or ten are gathered together in such oneness of faith and love that the eternal Christ does enter into the fellowship to transform the relationship and the persons involved. Your Church is now girding up its spiritual loins and making ready to mediate to you and your problem children the one Power that can dissolve away the fear and hate that causes social and mental illness.

The Church is facing the matter now with greater realism and understanding than ever before. It knows that there are many failures and partial successes for every truly successful case. It knows that there are conditions to be met before this divine healing power is released to man—that man must work out his own salvation or healing in so far as he is capable, in co-operation with the eternal Will; that he must grope and struggle and create agencies for the solution of these basic problems before running to God for help; that much of the slowness and failure to appropriate divine healing is due to God's withholding His aid until man develops and learns to work through these agencies, his own growth depending on these efforts; and that he must develop a mature quality of faith and love which sheer realism tells us only the few, at our present level of development, have attained. But the Church has now learned what every scientist knows—that the one successful experiment proves the point of reality, while the 100 or 1000 failures prove only a faulty technique. And now, when man has attained a high quality of social concern, has turned the power of his intellect and scientific method to the development of social welfare agencies, and has come to a new realization of the truth that all his institutions, like the Sabbath, were made for man, he is ready to receive the divine supplemental power that comes by faith and love. God gives wisely as well as generously. Had He given of His power before man could or would utilize it wisely and creatively, the healing gift would have produced a crippling dependency, stifling growth. Now, prayer is becoming a major instrument of the Church in helping her problem children resolve their difficulties.

With this knowledge we can take another look at our problem children with their delinquent or neurotic tendencies and recall that most of them believe in God and prayer and practice the latter more or less frequently, however ineffectually. Knowing also that fear and hate are such dominant forces within them, we must assume as a matter of reality that many cannot or will not rise to the heights of faith and love needed to transmit to them the full redemption of divine love. But we know that some do respond and are redeemed, healed, freed from their perversions, compulsions, and complexes in a manner that can be explained in no other way than by a divine, transforming love—the touch of the Master Physician—and that many more can and will so respond when we learn better how to pray and how to build around these deeply disturbed persons, or transmit to them, an atmosphere of healing faith and love. When the problem person is invited and integrated into the prayer fellowship composed of those who have attained mature faith and love, he becomes "charged," as it were, with the group atmosphere and may experience the transforming and enriching effect of divine love—of Christ in the fellowship.

"God is; and he is a rewarder of those who diligently seek him."[6] This was the ancient Hebrew theorem and corollary around which all the geometry of their souls was built. It is a twin affirmation and experience. Either God is not, or He is available to the experience of man. God cannot be retained as a rational hypothesis unless He is at times experienced as a redeeming, transforming, enriching Spirit within the life of man. Jesus opened wide to all who would enter the door of accessibility to God, which had stood ajar for the ancient prophet but which seemed closed to the masses of mankind. To the Church He delegated the privilege and responsibility of keeping that door open. Through the centuries, the Church has not done that job as well as it might, especially in keeping the way open for the problem children of the nations. Now the Church is awake. *In its new spirit of social concern, in its new concept of and emphasis on fellowship, in its more creative and realistic Christian education, in its utilization of and co-operation with other social agencies, in its pastoral counseling, and in its prayer groups, your Church is opening doors to make accessible to you and your problem children the divine power that is able to dissolve away the impediments and solve the problem.* Or, to change the figure of speech, your Church has assumed for itself the role of John the Baptist, who defined his mission as to "make straight the way," or to "make the crooked paths straight," for the One who would immediately follow and whose spiritual baptism would produce the real transformation of character. By utilizing to the full the insights and agencies of psychology and sociology, it is preparing to "make straight" the tangled, crooked paths of the mind (emotional complexes) until the problem child can respond with faith and love and so open channels to the infusion of divine love that frees, transforms, and enriches the inner life.

Your God is a Father who delights in giving good gifts to His children—His delinquent children, His neurotic children, His problem children of every description. He gives of Himself—the essence of which is divine love—"good measure, pressed down, . . . and running over." (Luke 6:38, K.J.V.) It is this divine infusion, this touch of eternity, that is needed to free your problem child of his own self-defeating forces. It is available to him if you can help him meet the conditions. In this task no other agency can be of as much assistance as your Church. Do not neglect it.

7.

The Pastor
as Counselor

THE ROLE OF THE CHURCH IN THERAPY and the counseling function of its ministers are honestly questioned by both professional and lay workers in religion and social service. Some do not understand it. A brief presentation of the essential nature of the counseling relationship should dispel these doubts and reveal why this specialized service is a natural and essential function of the Church. It was previously pointed out that many, if not most, problem children with tendencies toward delinquency or mental illness have difficulty fitting themselves into normal youth groups and group activities because of their feelings of alienation or compulsive aggressive tendencies, and that they need professional counseling service.

The well-known psychologist, Fritz Kunkel, wrote a very fine little book on adolescent psychology for the adolescent, entitled *My Dear Ego,* in which he describes the patterns of egocentricity most commonly expressed by teeners during their struggle toward maturity as "Star," "Bully," "Clinging Vine," and "Turtle." The development of the "We-experience" is presented as the antidote for egocentricity. To illustrate this Dr. Kunkel tells the story of eight boys on an all-afternoon hike taking the wrong turn and finding themselves far from home at 7:30 p.m. with no food and very hungry. One boy has an apple that none of the others knows about. This boy goes through a terrific struggle with temptation, trying to decide whether to drop back and eat it himself or divide it among the group. Finally the latter impulse wins and a true "We-experience" is born. Dr. Kunkel writes:

> The other seven boys are just as much refreshed and strengthened as is Henry. The We-experience is contagious. They did not stop to think especially about Henry's loyalty. Nobody asked him why he did not keep the apple for himself. They took his loyalty for granted, and that was very good. It destroyed the last chance of his ego to be proud of the performance. They did not know what was going on within him; they simply enjoyed the sharing of the last bit of food that came to them so unexpectedly. The result can be described as follows: One-eighth of a shared apple, plus the joy of the We-experience, is more than the whole apple plus the bad conscience of egocentricity.
>
> However, there is one objection: Someone might be egocentric without a bad conscience. He would enjoy the apple tremendously just because the others remained hungry. Then he would have the whole apple plus the whole egocentric joy, a malicious joy, to be sure, but anyhow joy. And in case of the sharing, he would only have one-eighth of an apple plus a tremendous regret that he was not clever enough to keep the whole for himself. The answer is that he still might have developed a stomach-ache, because his body did not share the egocentricity of his mind. But we cannot be sure of this. We have to admit that for some time he may be as well off as the one who shares the apple gladly. But soon his growing egocentricity will be caught in the vicious circle we discussed earlier.[1]

We will leave to the reader to find out for himself Dr. Kunkel's answer to this problem by reading *My Dear Ego*. The point we wish to make here is that the above quotation distinguishes those who mature normally from the problem child. The latter is he whose family relationships during childhood were so inadequate that he could not work through the "Star" or "Bully" or "Turtle" or "Clinging Vine" stage. He is too deeply enmeshed with his ego defenses, and the nature of his problem is too deeply hidden from himself. He "keeps messing up" and doesn't know why. The alienation of self from others is rather strong. He can't become a vital part of the fellowship, establish the "We-experience"—not by himself, that is; not without help. He needs a counselor. The Church is making provision for this need.

He really wants to be a part of the church fellowship, this problem youth, for deep down inside he does believe in God and in the Church. But for reasons he doesn't understand he just can't fit in with the group; so he may ridicule the whole idea. Similarly, he doesn't hate school as much as he pretends, but he hates himself and life because he just doesn't seem to fit. So he destroys school property, bullies other kids and the teacher, if possible, writes obscene notes, plays truant, or develops neurotic headaches to escape a social situation where he doesn't fit. The town builds playgrounds, ball fields, youth centers; the school develops a well-rounded extracurricular program; the church organizes a full social as well as religious activity schedule. The problem teener wrecks the playgrounds and rejects the programs. He is perverse. The public loses patience and yells, "Get tough with these delinquents." And church leaders are puzzled, wondering why they cannot reach those who most need what they are trying to give.

These kids are a little bit perverted. Their normal social impulses did become bent out of line during their growing-up years, because they were unable to form the wholesome childhood relationships essential to social development. Now they don't fit. They are the alienated. They can't, by themselves, form the "We-experience." They can't attain to true fellowship. And they are as puzzled as are the church workers and public authorities. It isn't punishment they need, but help. That which has become perverted (bent from its normal course) must become converted (redirected to its normal course). This can be accomplished only in the fellowship of normal persons, by attaining the "We-experience." Patient, persistent, understanding cultivation by the church youth worker can win many of them into the fellowship if they are accepted by the youth group. But many others are beyond this and need the help of a trained counselor. They have failed too often; resentment or anxiety is too deep; alienation is too complete. The untrained cannot cope with it.

Send them to the psychiatrist! Yes, but there are not enough psychiatrists available. Often it costs too much for most families. And psychiatrists aren't fully accepted by the not-too-well-informed public. (To make psychiatry more acceptable is also a role the Church can play better than most agencies.) But most of these problem children are not psychotic nor so deeply fixed in their perversions that professional psychiatry is essential. They do, however, need the help of a trained counselor. The Church today has recognized this need and is training its ministers to be counselors, to make counseling an essential part of pastoral service. In the church of today the minister is training himself professionally in order better to help the problem child (youth or adult) solve his essential problem. It has not been universally attained, but the movement is rapidly developing. Ministerial students in college and university are mastering the principles of psychology and mental health and the techniques of counseling. Many serve as intern chaplains in mental hospitals and prisons to gain clinical experience while studying pastoral counseling in seminary. Special summer courses are given to ministers for in-service training.

Let it be stated early in this discussion, and clearly, that the function of the pastor-counselor is not to replace psychiatry but to supplement and support it. He must be thoroughly trained for his work, able to recognize symptoms of deeper disturbances, particularly suicidal tendencies and cases that are beyond his power to cope with, and stand ready to refer these cases to the most adequate source of help. *But the minister who is thoroughly oriented in psychology and counseling technique, and as the appointed leader of the redeeming fellowship which is the Church, ought to be aware of his unique position and opportunity as a counselor and of the true therapy that is in his power to provide. Parents, teachers, and social workers should use him as a referral source.* The very recent trend in psychotherapy away from specific diagnosis and counselor-directed responses (and toward a permissive relationship that encourages free self-expression and self-awareness) has removed much of the danger which formerly existed in counseling with the deeply disturbed. They, the disturbed, set the pace and bring to

light the disturbing fears and resentments—self-directed or otherwise—as they are able to face them. The pastor-counselor is in a
unique position to establish with the client the kind of relationship
that makes this release and self-diagnosis possible and effective.

Some have expressed the feeling that a minister must have a dual
personality to be both preacher and counselor. His role as preacher
is positive and dynamic. He is proclaiming truth, imposing ideas,
arousing emotional response, attempting to persuade. He is often
dogmatic. As counselor he is also positive and dynamic, but he is
never dogmatic. He never proclaims or imposes or attempts to arouse
or persuade. He is the understanding listener who side by side with
his troubled counselee explores a problem life, and life. Together
they work through the meshes and road blocks—the one beset with
anxieties and resentments, the other abiding in faith and love.
Slowly the faith and love of the counselor weakens the fear and
hates of the counselee, a fellowship of two is established, and the
first breach is made in the wall of alienation. Then step by step
full social adjustment is attained. It does not require a dual personality to play these dual roles. But it does require a high degree
of freedom from one's own ego defenses and compulsive drives.
It requires certain personality traits that to a large degree are
acquirable, certain technical training, and the capacity of any good
actor, that of being able to appreciate and play different roles as
the occasion demands. The preacher can be persuasive and even
dogmatic in the pulpit because he is proclaiming not his own ideas
but eternal truths revealed by God and proved by thousands of
years of human experience. He is not projecting his own ego or ego
needs upon his listeners. It is, "Thus saith the Lord"; not, "Thus
crieth my ego." Thus the same man can, without any inner conflict, enter into the counseling relationship as listener (unobtrusive
guide without seeming to guide) and as searcher together with the
counselee for the answer to a particular problem.

Counseling is more an art than a science. It is the art of establishing a relationship. Like any art it rests upon certain techniques
and requires technical training. But technical training is not enough.
Of primary importance are the basic attitudes and sentiments of

the counselor. Does he have a deep and abiding faith in God, in life, in himself, and in his fellow man? Is he free of ego defenses and anxieties concerning his own role in life? Does he have a deep confidence in people, in their ability to work out their own problems in a permissive, not persuasive or restrictive relationship? Does he truly respect their right of self-direction? Is he deeply democratic in his interpersonal attitudes as well as in his consciously accepted political creed? Lacking in this the counselor will inevitably attempt to dominate the interview, to give too much advice, to be overly directive.

Also of primary importance is the matter of love, of loving one's neighbor as himself, and in both instances loving truly. It cannot be a piously assumed love that is a mask to hide from oneself his own ego disturbances. It must be a deep and basic concern and compassion for others, growing out of a deep sense of self-worth that, in turn, rests upon a true sense of divine forgiveness and acceptance—of oneness with God and with mankind through eternity. Thus one experiences himself and his fellow man as being of eternal and infinite worth. He can attain the generous response of forgiveness and acceptance of others as he has experienced it for himself. He can accept and love his counselee regardless of his faults and relative failures, because he has received from God absolute love and acceptance regardless of his own sins and imperfections. Having experienced God as eternal love, and having his own ability to love enhanced by divine love, he can feel love for his counselee, male or female, without its becoming focalized in genital desire or expression. It is free of sexual involvements by the counselor and is easily freed of sexual responses on the part of the counselee that may appear at certain stages. What other institution or agency exists, then, that can provide the public with adequately equipped counselors as can the Church through its technically trained and spiritually disciplined ministers?

The essential relationship between counselor and counselee is often spoken of as a state of empathy. The counselor "gets within" the other person, assumes the internal frame of reference of the counselee, perceives the counselee and his problem as he sees and feels himself and it. In a measure he feels what the counselee feels, but it is not full emotional identification, else it would not be a helpful relationship. Rather, the counselor feels how the counselee feels toward himself and others. He senses the anxieties and resentments and doubts of his client, but he does not share the same anxieties and resentments toward the original offending object, nor the same doubts toward the client which the client feels toward himself. He accepts the counselee's (client's) feelings as being understandable and legitimate, and he accepts the troubled person as a friend regardless of his trouble, but he is not crippled by the fear that the situation is hopeless. The counselor understands and accepts the counselee with his fears and hates, but he is not surrendered to them. He does not argue the needlessness of the other's feelings, nor does he lecture to him of faith and love. Rather, he helps clarify and drain off the excess emotion in an atmosphere of faith and love —of permissiveness.

Empathy, really, is the fundamental process in love. It is love in its broadest and deepest sense. It is a fully attained "We-experience"—a fellowship of two in a oneness of experience, with the wall of alienation momentarily breached. It is a love relationship that is positive and dynamic but that need not be expressed by words and will not be expressed genitally. It is a love (by the counselor) that does not threaten with punishment or rejection and which will not dominate or manipulate or use the other. It is the principal ingredient in the therapeutic relationship, for it casts out fear and overcomes hate, dissolves away the wall of alienation. It is that which speaks silently, saying, "I want you; I need you—yourself, your friendship, that which you have to share, you who are like all others yet unique—but I will not control you nor be controlled by you. Let us share deeply and freely of our inner selves, for we are both children of God."

The problem child (of whatever age) will not be able to accept this love at first. He (or she) has been hurt or disappointed or betrayed too many times. He is afraid to believe and accept such love and to project his feeling outward in response to it. He may fight desperately against it for a while, frequently decrying his unworthiness. He may even go out and commit another wrong to prove this unworthiness. He may show an extreme dependence upon the counselor, make too many demands, as an indirect method of securing proof of this love, assurance that it is dependable. If a woman, the counselee may at this point suggest or demand love's physical expression as proof of its reality. But the trained counselor who has come to terms with himself and his God, who is aware of his own inner needs and free of compulsive drives, who has a true experience of God as Love, can anticipate these demands of a troubled soul, refuse to be used by or to use the counselee in an unworthy manner, help her to a deeper understanding of love, and continue to love steadfastly without giving her a feeling of rejection. In this permissive atmosphere in which it is clear that the counselee's affection is accepted, wanted, needed, she slowly feels the threat removed, is able to form a true and enriching love relationship with the counselor, and in the light or confidence of that experience, can go out to form adequate relationships with others.

In the lives of most of our problem children, fear and hate have won over faith and love. Their aggressive and/or withdrawal, their dominative and/or submissive, tendencies are ruled by fear and hate rather than by faith and love. The primary function of the counselor is to permit a love relationship to develop between himself and his client in which his love brings out of hiding and strengthens the love capacities of the counselee to the point where he can love with confidence and slowly bring the old aggressive, dominative, withdrawal, or submissive impulses under the control of love. The job is not complete until the counselee has come to the experience of a divine love and acceptance which alone provides the supplement necessary for love to become the ruling force in his or her life. Then the individual is free of dependence upon the counselor—is free to be himself in the fullness of being.

In such a counselor-counselee relationship of complete acceptance, where all threat of rejection is removed, the deeply troubled person attains freedom to express his desires and needs, fears and hates. Following this emotional release come greater clarity of thought, truer insight with regard to self and its problems, and gradual self-acceptance. As he senses himself being accepted and loved regardless of his imagined or real shortcomings, he comes to a more realistic self-appraisal and feels free to accept and express his good and bad traits (verbally) without fear of rejection. Finally, then, he can look at his problem and make plans for solving it in a realistic manner. Realizing that love and acceptance are not dependent upon relative success or failure, he can face his problems of adjustment with renewed confidence and lessened fear, can face formerly baffling situations as soluble problems, and can make decisions. Through all of this the counselor listens, understands, loves, and accepts. Much of the time he is silent. Often he reflects back the counselee's feelings and attitudes. This in itself is an aid to clarification without being at all expository. Only occasionally does he give explanation or provide information, for he trusts implicitly in the counselee's right and ability to work out his own solution in this permissive relationship. And his confidence is silently conveyed to the counselee. When empathy, or the love relation, is thoroughly established, and especially during the planning stage of the interviews, the counselor may be more direct in giving information or making recommendations. For by then the counselee is able to accept or reject information without the panicky fear of being rejected and without sinking back into the morass of dependency. It is the relationship that is of primary importance. The technique, while important, is secondary.

Following a long quotation from a paper written by one of his staff counselors, Mr. Oliver H. Brown, in which the counselor-client relationship was presented as a "love" relationship, Carl Rogers says:

> Here in this highly personal material is a reaching out— both on the part of the therapist and on the part of the client— for a new type of formulation of the process of therapy. It is not easily understood, and reactions to it seem to be strong. It is, as far as our own group is concerned, still in an infant and groping stage. It is clear, however, that the stress is upon a direct experiencing in the relationship. The process is not seen as primarily having to do with the client's memory of his past, nor

with his exploration of the problems he is facing, nor with the perception he has of himself, nor with the experiences he has been fearful of admitting into awareness. The process of therapy is, by these hypotheses, seen as being synonymous with the experiential relationship between client and therapist. Therapy consists in experiencing the self in a wide range of ways in an emotionally meaningful relationship with the therapist. The words—of either client or counselor—are seen as having minimal importance compared with the present emotional relationship which exists between the two.[2]

The writer, through many years of counseling experience, has "groped" his way into and through some of the difficulties and dangers of the above type of counselor-client relationship. He can testify to these difficulties and dangers. But he has also experienced the effectiveness of that relationship as the key to the solution of serious problems of adjustment, whether the basic symptoms run toward delinquency or mental illness. His position as pastor, as minister of religion (faith and love), has been most helpful in establishing this right kind of emotional relationship.

Christ established the Church as the agency or body or fellowship through which his redemptive work would be progressively extended through history. He is an ever-present quality within that fellowship, to be experienced as divine love by those who have become true members of the body. He, His love, is the therapeutic power that brings healing (redemption) to the problem child of God. It is His redemptive love that can free the delinquent or neurotic from the resentments and anxieties that have enslaved him, and which provides the divine supplement that enables him henceforth to be ruled by love. If his fears and resentments, his exaggerated aggressive or withdrawal tendencies, have kept him from responding to the call of love and becoming a part of the redeeming fellowship, it is the spiritually mature minister of the church, who, because he has experienced this redeeming love and disciplined himself in the art of counseling, is best qualified to establish the above-described counseling relationship, break down the wall of alienation, and guide the troubled person into the larger redemptive fellowship of the Church. Toward this end the Church is training its ministers to serve its problem children.

There are approximately 240,000 Protestant ministers in our American churches. Many of these now have, and in the very near future most will have, prepared themselves to serve their constituents in this effective counseling relationship. These men are training themselves to recognize characteristic symptoms of the few who have so completely surrendered to their fears and hates, their flights from reality, or their perversions, that institutional care or psychiatric treatment is necessary. These they will refer to the proper source of help. And if these seriously disturbed persons will not accept this needed professional service, they will try to establish such a relationship of trust and love as we have been describing (provide a needed supportive therapy) until enough of the counselee's fear and distrust has been removed that he will accept the institutional and psychiatric treatment that may be required. On the other hand, there are the many problem persons whose behavior patterns may be described as delinquent or neurotic, but who are not deeply perverted or psychotic. These can be helped best by the trained pastor-counselor himself through the kind of counselor-counselee relationship described above. The tendency in such counseling is away from diagnosis and prolonged psychoanalysis, which formerly was often in advance of the client's readiness to face the problem factors. Rather, the counselor creates an empathic relationship of full acceptance and permissiveness that permits the client to do his own diagnosis and analysis in accordance with his growing readiness to look at himself and accept himself. Thus there is little or no danger of hurt to the client. If no progress is noted after a reasonable time, then referral can be made to a more likely source of help.

Jesus was the perfect counselor. His love and faith were perfect, fully matured. He could establish complete empathy with the problem person. Love between the Master Counselor and the counselee was perfect. He knew what was in the heart of man and needed no one to tell him.[3] He, the Christ, could sense and feel perfectly the fear and hate and guilt that burdened the mind of the afflicted. And He could, with His perfect faith, lift that burden to His Father and find it being lifted from His own soul and that of the troubled person at the same time. They had become truly one in shared guilt and forgiveness or freedom.

The Christian pastor-counselor cannot love so perfectly nor respond with such perfect faith. But he can love the problem person in all his perverseness and neuroticism, because he can see him and respond to him as he will be when freed from his disturbance. He can experience deeply in empathy (love) the emotional disturbances of the counselee, but he experiences this upon a background of his own deep sense of forgiveness and restored divine fellowship, and upon the ability to love even his enemy, the unlovable. He can experience and respond to his counselee, even during his most troubled period, as he will be when cured (made whole) and be to him the kind of friend he then can be. In this atmosphere of love and confident anticipation the healing process moves forward. Often unconsciously, usually non-verbally, at least during the early phases of the counseling relationship, the eternal Christ is experienced in this process and the counselor-client relationship becomes a little koinonia that leads to the larger Christian fellowship and complete readjustment or redemption. The counselor-counselee relationship— where every thought, feeling, frustration, and desire is shared—is of such an intimate nature that the presence of that Other needs to be recognized and experienced. His perfect love is needed as a supplementing force to safeguard the relationship, to enrich it and keep it of the mind and spirit. *The Church, through its redeemed, consecrated, and technically trained ministry is the one institution that can supply the counseling service needed to supplement the also needed work of the psychiatrist and social case worker.*

The Church and its ministry, however, look upon counseling as an instrument of prevention of serious problem developments. Thus pastoral counseling is now centering very largely in the area of family relationships. Many books and booklets have been written recently to guide the minister in the premarriage conference and in dealing with family conflict situations. Church organizations, denominationally and interdenominationally, conduct seminars for in-service training of their ministers in premarital and marital counseling. Short summer courses are given by seminaries in various locales. In conjunction with its program of education for better family living, the Church is concentrating on its counseling service in this area to help work out the problems before the crises occur. By this it is determined to reduce greatly the incidence of divorce and to help married couples make marriage the enriching relationship it was designed by God to be.

Greater and greater numbers of church youth are not only given courses on preparation for marriage but are encouraged to counsel with their pastors weeks or months in advance of their wedding plans. This trend is expected to reach near universality among our church youth in the near future. Different ministers follow different procedures, but each tries to cover all the factors that are known to affect marriage as thoroughly as time and circumstances permit. It is far from universal at present. Many couples still run to a minister at the last minute, wanting to be married immediately. Others come with plans already made, and time only for one or two conferences. But the trend is away from this hurry-up type of thing. When premarital counseling becomes the established custom among our youth, marital difficulty and delinquency will show a marked decline.

The Reverend Warren D. Bowman, Minister of Washington City Church of the Brethren, Washington, D.C., has this to say in his booklet *Counseling With Couples Before Marriage:*

> It is quite important to get the couple for the first conference from four to six weeks, or even earlier, before the wedding, and to guide them in the pursuance of a training course for marriage. When the conference takes place a few days or a few hours before the wedding there is not sufficient time to supply the gaps in their information, or to correct wrong attitudes, and they are apt to go into marriage ill-prepared. . . . A conference prior to the engagement is quite desirable as the minister has the opportunity to help the two young people determine whether they are really in love and well suited to each other. He can direct their thinking relative to the problems that should be solved before they become engaged, and as to the desirable length of engagement in their specific case.

During the premarriage conference, which is usually from one to two hours in length, several scientific and genuinely Christian books which deal specifically with the various adjustments that will need to be made for a successful marriage should be placed in the hands of the couple. They should be advised to study these books very carefully before the wedding and to make note of any questions that arise in their minds that they would like to discuss further with their pastor. There should always be an opportunity for the couple to come to their pastor with additional questions after they have studied the prescribed books on marital adjustment.[4]

Dr. Bowman discusses all or most of the following questions with couples during the premarriage conferences:

1. How long have you known each other?
2. Are you really in love?
3. What do your families think of your marriage?
4. How do your ages correspond?
5. Is there anything in the personality of either of you that might hinder marital happiness?
6. What are your plans for growth in love?
7. What attitude will you take toward difficulties that may arise?
8. What kind of friends will you have?
9. Have you had a physical examination?
10. What economic plans have you made?
11. What are your plans for living accommodations?
12. Have you discussed the matter of children?
13. Do you possess adequate information relative to physical adjustment in marriage?
14. What part will religion play in your marriage?

Some pastor-counselors have the couple fill out a questionnaire at the first session. The writer does not follow this practice, preferring a more informal procedure. If he feels that the situation warrants, and if the couple request it after the matter is discussed, a personality inventory type of test is given and/or a sex information test. In most cases these instruments are not necessary. Often they are helpful. In our premarriage conferences we cover as thoroughly as time and need permit six broad areas that I call keys to happy marriage. If they score par on all of these they are told half jokingly and half seriously that they will be given a written guarantee of a happy marriage. The further stipulation is added that in case of serious friction they must come for counseling before it becomes too serious and that even though there is no apparent trouble a "1000 mile" checkup will be expected.

We are not offering in this chapter a course on counseling, but we are pointing out a trend and development. It is a service the modern church is preparing to give to the people of its constituency, because such service is inherent in Christian love. It is a primary function of religion. Furthermore, the pastor's concern and counseling does not end with the wedding. Having received premarital counseling and knowing the nature of the counseling service they may have if needed, many couples will return to the minister who married them, or to another, if serious difficulties arise. Sometimes the writer exacts this promise from the couple previous to marriage. This is usually done in cases where the counseling period has been all too brief. Such a promise is hardly necessary when adequate counseling has occurred.

Problems arise in all families—problems between husband and wife, between children and parents, and among the children. Most families are able to solve their problems, to muddle through or work through without too much conflict and distress. But sometimes they get stuck with a conflict situation that won't work out. They need help. In the past most families tried to hide their failures from their minister. They wanted him always to see them at their best and to believe the best of them. Now they are learning that the minister knows that even the finest people often have serious problems, and they are beginning to accept him as the person who is best prepared to help them with their problems. This is a development, a trend, not a full attainment.

The particular pattern of conflict and tension varies with every family situation. But the basic elements usually derive from failure in one or another of the "keys" described above. Perhaps emotional (ego) immaturity is the factor that wrecks or cripples more marriages than anything else. The man or woman so afflicted needs supportive therapy for a time in the atmosphere of the type of counselor-counselee relationship described earlier in this chapter. Only in this permissive, empathic relationship of full acceptance will the immature adult be able to surrender his defenses, face himself with true insight, and be able to accept himself. From this point on he (or she) can be "guided" in the growth of a mature Christian love and faith that is expressed adequately in enriching family and social relationships. The pastor-counselor who is well-oriented in psychology and rooted in the Christian fellowship is best equipped to help salvage the marriage that is failing, for the failure is largely a failure in love. Back of him and standing by to aid in salvaging the home is his Church, the redeeming fellowship of love. Taking the problem family into its fold, the Church makes easier the release of love and faith on their part and the re-establishment of a satisfying relationship.

It has been emphasized repeatedly that most problem children come from problem homes. Love failed in the life of the child because it had failed in the lives of the parents and in the family relationship. The church that has a sense of its mission as a redeeming fellowship and which is able to hold or win to its fellowship the disturbed children from problem homes will be able to save many of them from becoming serious problem personalities by being a second family for them. As was shown in chapter 4, the church has access to most of these at least, until the conflict has become prolonged and severe. The church that is oriented to see the signs and report the cases of disturbed children, and the pastor who is oriented in counseling procedure, can hold or win a large proportion of these who in the past have drifted away from its influence. The church and its minister, more than any other institution or counselor, has the freedom to go to the home, make the problem family aware of its problem, and point the way to a solution. Though no counseling can be effective while there is no readiness for it, the minister is in the best position to create that readiness. His concern is God's concern, and it can be so presented. He is still obedient to his commission: "Go out into the highways and the byways and bring them in."[5] And in this obedience he will not be working alone. The guiding Spirit still works with those attuned to His will and His work.

This process of healing—moral, mental, and sometimes physical—often is brought about in the counseling relationship by the pastor-counselor who functions as described above and who has learned to utilize prayer and suggestion effectively in the counseling relationship. Often the pastor-counselor literally prays his way into the mind and heart of the counselee, to establish a high quality of empathy, long before his interest is known to the counselee and discussed openly. The pastor-counselor learns to detect a state of readiness for prayer, to help develop that state by the quality of his own faith and love and previous praying, and to form with the counselee a fellowship of healing prayer at the appropriate time. A few whose love and faith are so great and whose personalities are so compelling are able to create that state of readiness at first contact, especially if they are known to and regarded highly by the troubled persons. Such cases were common in the ministry of Jesus. His love and faith were so perfect, His personality so compelling, and the people had learned to expect so much of Him! It is not so in the experience of most of His followers. Weeks or months of cultivation, of softening, are required to create a state of readiness and an atmosphere of faith. But the pastor who has learned to use prayer effectively in the counseling relationship and who is backed by a prayer fellowship in his church will be found to be the most effective helper available for the prevention or cure of the delinquent or the mentally ill.

8.

The Church and Its Allies

TOMORROW THE CHURCH AND THE STATE will dominate the whole field of social service. The agencies they support will form a partnership of co-operative service. Each is dedicated to the welfare of all the people. Working at different levels or areas of need but in full co-ordination, they will be able to provide adequate living for all. The failure of a single person or family is a blemish upon the Church and the State. The size and diversity of interests of both have tended to make them ponderous, and ponderously slow to respond to specific problem situations. To fill a gap of unmet need, various private agencies have risen and are rendering a valuable service. These are allied with church and public agencies in the local community where problem cases are community problems—failures in community living. The motive that underlies their work is spiritual; the service, religious. It has sprung directly or indirectly from the Church and is the concern of the Master.

"I came that they may have life, and have it abundantly," said the Master of life.[1] This was His purpose, and it is the mission of the Church which He established as His institutional body to implement and perpetuate that concern. He had in mind, I believe, our problem children, in whose lives the channel of abundant living has become clogged or choked off. His was the greatest social concern ever expressed. "It is not the well but the sick who need the physician," He reminded the people of His day. And He healed the sick—the physically, the mentally, the morally, and the socially sick. The "publican" and the "sinner," the socially alienated of His day, were gathered into the fellowship of His disciples. To bring this purpose into fruition Jesus served directly in all areas of basic human need. He fed the multitudes, setting the example that man's material needs are a part of the abundant life. He healed the sick, setting the example that health is a part of the good life. He taught His matchless parables to the crowds at the gates of the Temple, in the market place, on the hillside or by the seashore, setting the example that education and cultural values are essential to the fullness of life. He chatted with the throngs in the market places, entertained at the wedding feast, and was the popular guest on dinner occasions, calling attention to the reality of man's social or fellowship needs. He forgave sins, restored man to a sense of divine acceptance, and released to him the dynamic of divine love by which he could attain the moral and spiritual mastery supremely essential to abundant living.

The Church has remained true to her Master in the main, though falling far short, in making these same provisions for abundant living. It was first in alms, first to raise large sums of money for the poor and needy. The disciples carried on the healing ministry of Jesus, and the Church has ever been in the lead in sending her nurses and medical missionaries to the far places of the world, not to mention the hospitals built and administered in the name of the Great Physician. A few great universities existed for the privileged, but it was the Church that built schools for the common people, to dispel the darkness of ignorance and superstition. While incomplete conversion has permitted fear, guilt, envy, greed, jealousy, prejudice, and other divisive forces to mar its fellowship, the Church has always held up the ideal of brotherhood and the universal fellowship in which there is no class or race distinction—in which there is "neither Jew nor Greek, there is neither bond nor free, there is neither male nor female." (Galatians 3:28, k.j.v.) And it has done more than any other institution to break down these artificial walls of alienation. In the realm of the moral and spiritual it stands supreme.

Two things happened along the course of history that made other help necessary: (1) The job got too big for the imperfect Church. Too many "giants inhabited the land" of human need. It backed off, failed to go forward "to possess the promised land," empowered and guided by the divine Hand. (2) It took on too much of an "other world" interest and emphasis, drawing too sharp a contrast between the "spiritual" and the more mundane affairs and needs, overemphasizing the former and neglecting the latter. Other agencies had to step in to breach the gap. The State took over the chief burden of education, and later economic relief, taxing the public to compel support that would not be voluntarily given. Federal, state, and municipal support is given to hospitals. And literally scores of public and private nonsectarian agencies have sprung up to help meet the varied needs of problem people. Social welfare is an inherent interest and function of the Church, as vital to its life as evangelism and Christian education. But it is not a function of the Church alone. The Church recognizes and needs these other agencies as allies. It recognizes many of them as its children or stepchildren. Whether associated with or dissociated from the Church, it is the Spirit resident within the Church that gave birth to and provides the dynamic that sustains most of these. Consciously or unconsciously, openly recognized or disguised by their staff workers, these agencies are rendering a vitally needed service in the spirit, if not the "name," of the Master Servant of man. The responsibility for the welfare of our problem children is that of the state and community, and it is the prophetic ministry of the Church ever to call the state and community to their responsibility. State agencies and state co-ordination and supervision will always be needed. Many of the private, nonsectarian agencies will continue for many years to render valuable service and some may continue indefinitely. But as the Church recovers its rightful position in this its own inherent field of service, and it is doing this quite rapidly, fewer of these other private agencies will be necessary. The Church-supported and state agencies will be left as the major allies. In meeting the challenging problems of our problem folk, we need the courts and police, the probation office, the service clubs, the schools, and social service agencies both public and private; we need the professionally trained social worker, the psychologist, and the psychiatrist.

As suggested in the previous chapter, counseling plays a central role in problem solving. The individual or family that has become deeply enmeshed in a complication of problems needs and wants personal help. The most serious of these will require full psychiatric treatment, sometimes within the controlled environment of a special institution. But the majority of our seriously disturbed individuals (neurotic or delinquent) and families do not require psychiatry, and it would not be available to all of them in the forseeable future if they did. They do, however, need a highly professional counseling service that can be provided by the trained minister, the university counseling center, the larger high school, the city YMCA, and numerous private counseling centers, particularly those specializing in marriage counseling.

Since the majority of young couples are married in the Church and ministers are rapidly preparing themselves professionally for the function of marital counseling, in the very near future most marriage counseling will be done by the minister or staff counselor of the local church or by a central counseling service of a local Council of Churches. But at present this service is not available to the majority of people through their churches, so other agencies have come into being to meet the need. Perhaps some will always be needed, but never will they be able to meet the total need. The churches must and will, in the near future, carry the major load, but in the meantime they must become acquainted with these allied services and direct their problem families to them when the needs arise.

The report of the 1948 National Conference on Family Life revealed that there were about 300 marriage and family counseling centers in active service, spread over 40 of the 48 states. The American Association of Marriage Counselors is a professional organization composed of qualified practitioners in this field, counselors who meet its detailed requirements. It conducts conferences and clinical sessions and engages in research and promotional activities, aiming at high standards of professional proficiency. The National Council on Family Relations is a sort of national clearing house, an educational and promotional organization. It does not conduct marriage counseling centers but fosters more adequate counseling services. The Planned Parenthood Federation of America maintains an organization in most cities and provides information, medical consultation, and limited premarital and postmarital counseling, particularly as related to the sexual aspect of marriage. The National Association for Mental Health has initiated the establishment of mental hygiene and child guidance clinics in many areas of the country, where trained child psychologists, social caseworkers, and psychiatrists help the more seriously disturbed children and parents solve their basic problems. Your church leaders are acquainted with the work of these allied agencies and stand ready to direct your problem child or neighbor to the nearest and most adequate source of help.

The Family Service Association of America has member agencies in most cities throughout the country. In large cities they have a central office and branch agencies. Casework services involving prolonged marriage counseling are provided. Homemaking instruction and supervision is often given, and sometimes emergency financial help is made available. Emily Hartshorne Mudd describes the Family Service of Los Angeles Area as follows:

Staff. The professional casework staff of twenty-two persons operate from six different district offices. They are all graduates of an accredited school of social work and the majority have five or more years of casework experience. All workers are supervised, and psychiatric consultation seminars and discussion groups are available to staff. A panel of psychoanalysts has been developed in co-operation with the psychiatric consultant.

Clients. To date, there has been no emphasis on premarital counseling. Approximately one-third of the families using Family Service present some marital conflict. Services are available only to persons in the Los Angeles area.

Method and Philosophy. During the initial period of exploration, from three to five interviews, the caseworkers attempt to understand the various manifestations of the problem and help the client clarify his concept of it. (1) It is determined whether help in the environmental area must be given before the marital problem can even be touched on. (2) Possibilities for bringing the other partner into counseling are explored through the client recognizing his problem as marital difficulty. He may then tell the partner of seeking counseling, or plan to bring the partner into participation with the agency. (3) If the partner does not participate, work can be with the client only. Following the exploratory period, a plan may be established with one or both partners to continue for a specified period of time. Joint interviews may be used at certain stages.

Fee. There is a sliding fee scale ranging from $1 to $3 per interview for those who are able to pay. [The fee scale has since been changed to a maximum of $10 per interview, with no additional charge for more than one interview in any week.]

Length of Contact. Interviews are scheduled for forty-five minutes, usually at weekly intervals. The average length of contact is three months and ranges from those situations that require only one interview to those where contact lasts for six months or longer.[2]

Describing the Marriage Council of Philadelphia, of which she is executive director and which carried a staff of two full-time and three part-time counselors with on-call psychiatric service and consultation, the same writer states:

Method and Philosophy. The council attempts to offer the client a positive and dynamic approach to his problem which may result in a better understanding of self, greater assurance, and an enhanced capacity to live adequately in his marriage. Counselors recognize that it takes time for people to change, to grow, and to make adjustments. Therefore, patience, warmth, and understanding, sympathy without indulgence, and tolerance are used to support the client in his effort to adjust. The goal of counseling is to help people over the spots that seem rough to them, and so enable them to grow, develop, and handle their own problems.[3]

Though details of organization and operation vary from place to place, similar counseling services are available in most metropolitan areas. Churches within a wide radius of these centers are becoming acquainted with the type of service offered, are promoting those services and utilizing them more and more, helping them in their redemptive function. Social problems, family problems, the problems that make for delinquency and/or mental illness are complex and rooted in a variety of relationships. The co-operation of several agencies is often helpful or necessary in arriving at an adequate solution. Such co-operation between the Church and other community agencies is illustrated by the following case in which the writer participated.

John and Cora (we shall call them) were about 40 years old and had been married 18 years. They had a boy aged 17 and a girl almost 16. Five other children ranged from 12 to $1\frac{1}{2}$ years, and Cora was then pregnant (at the time I became involved with the case). They lived in a four-room "flat" in a very poor neighborhood. The house was usually in a very "messy" condition and Cora was dowdy, often slovenly, in appearance. John, in speech, expression, and general bearing, revealed a deep-seated inferiority complex; but he dressed up and made a fairly neat appearance when he went out. He fought with Cora over the "messy" condition of the house and she with him over lack of adequate support. They had separated twice for brief periods, and he had spent several months in a mental hospital.

John was a skillful auto mechanic, though very slow at his work. This contributed partly to his frequent periods of unemployment. Another and greater cause was his drinking bouts. He was a more or less typical alcoholic with periodic binges occurring every two to three months, the intervening period being characterized by repentance and self-condemnation. The oldest boy had been involved in two episodes that brought police action. In the second he was taken to Juvenile Court but released without being officially charged with delinquency. The girl, quite attractive, was in constant conflict with her father regarding her dating problems and irresponsibility at home. The family had been on and off public assistance since its inception and were alternately on the active and inactive files of Family Service. Cora and the older girls were members of a small church in the neighborhood, and the younger children attended its

Sunday school. John would not attend their church because it was "too radical" to suit him. He had formerly been a member of a Presbyterian church. He came to me for help one night, after a big family fight, in a deeply depressed mood.

Here was a situation that required much circumstantial adjusting, psychotherapy, and a more vital utilization of religious faith and love. There could be no fully satisfactory solution. Innate weakness would continue to make adequate adjustment very difficult if not impossible. These were a sample of "God's awkward children." John was a bit of a psychopathic personality; Cora was dull-normal in intellect and low in ambition; the oldest boy was also a little dull; the girl, talented but lazy; and the younger children, bewildered. A whole community was involved in bringing about stabilization and some degree of adequacy.

The writer's job as pastor-counselor was first to establish a strong empathic relationship and provide ego support that would hold John steady during the initial stage, then help him attain emotional release, insight, and self-acceptance. He was encouraged to join a local unit of Alcoholics Anonymous, become a member of our church, and join the choir. Though his voice was not particularly good, he could sing tenor. These activities provided fellowship, a sense of acceptance, and some degree of worth. The church attended by the other members of the family was asked to help them similarly. The girl was used as a pianist. Family Service reactivated the case, gave some emergency material assistance in connection with the birth of the child, and over a period of several months gave homemaking and child care counsel, not only in regard to the baby but in establishing a better mother-child relationship with the other children. The writer also counseled with the oldest boy and girl. Through the help of local service organizations the girl and two younger children were sent to a church camp and the boy was given a battery of tests and vocational counseling at the YMCA Testing Bureau. These same service clubs helped the boy and girl obtain part-time work. A difficult job was done with a fair measure of success.

The fact that the people of the community were sincerely concerned about them was one of the strongest redeeming factors. This was something different than merely receiving help from the hands of paid employees of a public agency doing their official duty. To give one's "body to be burned" or to give away all the public funds to aid the needy without love being expressed in the interpersonal relationship profits very little. But when the people of the community feel and express true concern through organized and intelligent effort, the problem person begins to feel that love and acceptance, and it gives him a new sense of worth and a new motivation and dynamic for making a better adjustment.

A large percentage of American families live in towns and rural communities removed from the metropolitan centers and from the services of many of the agencies described above. In such an area a plan is being promoted that has great potentialities. The concerned people of these communities believe that service should be a personal and co-operative relationship in which the local community organizations carry the major burden of the service activities, with the state supplementing, co-ordinating, and supervising through its public assistance program and a representative from the Department of Welfare. While interest and activity will center on the prevention of delinquency and mental illness, activities will relate to the total welfare needs of the respective communities. In each county or larger population center, a community council or welfare association is formed, carrying the community name and composed of representatives from local churches or ministerial groups, the schools' Parent-Teacher Associations, service clubs, American Association of University Women in some instances, and existing social service organizations, including Public Health and Public Assistance. This central council or association will study local conditions and promote activities designed to alleviate needs.

The principle and policy of volunteerism will be utilized to the full, volunteers being recruited from the various organizations, given in-service training, and assigned to work with existing welfare agencies and institutions and to supplement the work of these agencies as needed. A list of prospective foster homes will be kept on file and parents who take a dependent or delinquent child, providing a temporary foster home, will be given counseling if desired—this to remove the fear many people have of trying to cope with the problems of the problem child. In co-operating with Public Assistance and whatever other social welfare agencies that may exist, groups from co-operating organizations, particularly churches, will seek out socially isolated or problem families and persons and try to integrate them into wholesome group activities, bringing them into a redeeming fellowship. Similar groups will visit regularly such institutions as mental hospitals and schools for delinquents that are not too distant, not merely to "put on" programs for the inmates but to conduct fellowship activities with them. Selected inmates will participate with the visiting groups in the conducting of worship services, dramatic productions, group recreation, and service projects such as sewing for the needy, etc. Finally, this central council or association will promote short courses and the utilization of reading materials on better family living.

The central and perhaps key factor in the whole program as being planned is an adequate counseling service that begins in the public schools. All teachers would be requested to take sufficient work in mental hygiene to understand better the problem child and to be able to recognize problem symptoms before they become too acute. Local school systems are requested to designate certain teachers, who have taken or will take courses in counseling, as student counselors and give them sufficient time from teaching duties for this function. These counselors would help students with their problems of educational, vocational, social, and family adjustment, referring the more serious problem cases to other sources of help. Also the schools are requested to make provision for short courses on "Teenage Problems" for the pupils at the junior high and senior high levels.

To supplement this service, referrals will be made to trained social workers in Public Assistance or some other welfare agency. The State Employment office may provide supplementary aptitude testing and vocational counseling. The Big Brother-Big Sister program of utilizing business and professional men and women (and housewives who are professionally trained) as volunteer lay counselors will be tried, each taking a boy or girl upon referral and helping work out the problem of adjustment. Some of these would serve as volunteer probation officers under court supervision. For the more deeply disturbed, who require psychotherapy but not necessarily full psychiatric treatment, the state is being urged to enlarge the facilities of university counseling centers or psychiatric clinics, with extension service to outlying communities, and to institute a system of traveling therapists (counselors) who will set up office one day a week in the various communities. The cost of this service would be borne partly by the state, partly by fees, and partly by local subscription. In some places a minister or school official who has specialized in psychology and psychotherapy will be able to take care of these more serious problem cases. With such extended counseling services, a very few psychiatrists in state hospitals and private practice can handle those few who are so seriously and deeply disturbed that psychiatric treatment is necessary.

Such movements are just beginning to function, but they hold great promise. They are long-term programs that will require many years to perfect. But with churches actively promoting and initiating, as many are now beginning to do, and with the state co-operating with supplemental and supervisory services, many of the most valuable features can be brought to fruition within a reasonably short time.

In Illinois we find a splendid example of such co-operation between local community organizations and state institutions, with the effective use of volunteer workers. Much more can be done. These activities have been variously reported in numerous publications. *The Kiwanis Magazine* carried the story under the title, "Climate of Hope," written by Richard E. Gosswiller. He wrote:

> In an old people's ward at Manteno State Hospital for the mentally ill, Manteno, Illinois, a housewife in a pink smock bends over a large white crib and serves the noon meal to a tired woman of eighty . . . In a men's ward, a Kiwanian, wearing an arm band, listens as a patient tells about his brother in Chicago who never visits. . . . In a woman's ward, a young girl, who sometimes has delusions of grandeur, watches while three

pink-clad housewives entertain around the piano. In answer to a direct question, she exclaims—quite humbly: "The volunteers are wonderful! When I get out of here, I want to be one myself."

The volunteers are people from outside the mental hospital who devote part of their time to helping the people within. At Illinois State Hospitals, they are members of the Volunteer Service Program; the letters VSP are imprinted on the women's pink smocks and on the arm bands of the men. The volunteers represent the community: They are intermediates between society and the sick. They offer compassion, understanding—even friendship—to people who, not so many years ago, were both feared and forgotten. Their numbers are growing. Today, many hospitals throughout Canada and the United States encourage volunteer programs. In three states—Minnesota, Texas and Illinois—volunteer activities are coordinated at the state level. . . .

By far the greatest number of volunteers at Manteno come as groups. Altogether, fifty-two organizations representing fifteen communities in Illinois visit the hospital from two to six times a year to entertain and provide companionship for patients. One of these groups is the Manteno Sub-Deb Club, composed of forty-five teen-age girls. Another is the Kiwanis Club of Park Forest.

About once every six weeks, on a Saturday afternoon, five to ten Park Forest Kiwanians visit Meyer 1, a large ward for men at Manteno. They bring with them refreshments, but more important, they bring reassurance that the patients are not forgotten, that someone outside does care.[4]

In this same article, the writer quotes Dr. Otto L. Bettag as follows:

After a demonstration period that began in September 1951, the Volunteer Services Program, financed by a grant from the Field Foundation, was permanently incorporated into the Illinois Department of Public Welfare in September 1953. I have followed closely the work of the 5000 volunteers who come regularly to serve the 48,000 patients at our eleven state hospitals for the mentally ill and the two schools for the mentally deficient. The Volunteer Services Program is one of the latest aspects in modern psychiatric treatment. In Illinois, it has attracted outstanding civic, church, service and social organizations.[5]

This quotation is given largely to show that it has become officially recognized that friendship, love, and acceptance by the people of a community are vital factors in the prevention and cure of mental illness. The same applies to delinquency, and the type of program described above can operate even more effectively in schools for delinquents, even prisons, than in mental hospitals. Furthermore, the volunteer social welfare organization in the local community, composed of a truly concerned citizenry with a few professionally trained persons to guide, can institute a service that will help the majority of problem families and individuals attain satisfactory community living and thus prevent vast numbers from having to be committed to the above-type institutions. After all, delinquency and mental illness are largely symptoms of a failure in community living. The prevention and cure resides in the community—in the community that loves, accepts, and reintegrates these alienated persons back into its life. It is the responsibility of the whole community; but the local church, which is the larger family and the smaller community, the special fellowship in which human love is enriched with divine love, has a central role to play. This role the Church has accepted. And many of you who read this will find that your church is taking its place as a major healing force in the life of the community.

As a further illustration of the need and opportunity for cooperative community action in helping our problem children, I shall briefly present the matter of probation. Criminal law developed primarily to protect life and property. Offenders against the laws were punished as a matter of justice. Courts of justice evolved as worthy institutions of a society imbued with a sense of justice, basic in moral and social development. But the problem of weighing out justice justly has always been a thorny one.

Probation is a system of social investigation and supervisory treatment of convicted offenders in an attempt at social rehabilitation within the environment of a normal community life. The court imposes certain restrictions for guidance and protection and assigns a trained officer to serve as guide. It is much more than mere leniency. It is an attempt to individualize justice and make it curative. The judge often bases his decision as to disposal of the case on the probation officer's investigation and report, and if the offender is not committed to an institution the probation serves as his social crutch for a designated period. Firm but friendly supervision and guidance are given.

Like any new system or procedure for dealing with complex problems, probation has been only relatively successful. But the relative degree of success is steadily increasing. Much had to be learned in principle and practice. Officers could not be provided as rapidly as the need and demand developed. Political manipulation and public impatience because of failures were impediments. Too often probation officers were merely firm supervisors rather than friendly, understanding, empathic counselors. Too frequently the probationer could not or would not accept the probation officer in his true role, but looked upon him as an official representative of the society toward which his resentment and aggressive impulses were particularly directed.

The relative failure of the probation system is basically a failure in establishing an adequate counseling relationship of empathy or, if you please, love. It is not a matter of a trained social caseworker making an accurate diagnosis of the social and psychological factors involved and prescribing a course of action, although such training should be a part of the equipment of the probation officer. Probation is a system for the implementation of love in the treatment of social offenders—love revealing its two sides: its firm, disciplining side of justice and its tender, healing side of mercy. To be fully effective it must be operated by persons motivated by love and able to express love purely and wisely. The adequate relationship between the probation officer and probationer is that of the counselor-counselee relationship described in the preceding chapter. It is a therapeutic relationship involving supportive therapy, emotional release, insight, self-acceptance, and realistic planning, which can be achieved only through such relationship. The Church is making available to the courts the consecrated men and women best equipped to establish this relationship.

Except in cases of deeply fixed perversions, which are relatively few and seldom placed on probation, the deeply concerned lay counselor who serves as a volunteer with the court is often the most effective worker in the social rehabilitation of the young offender— your problem child and mine. It is easier for him to establish rapport and empathy with the suspicious problem child. His is not a paid service or a professional duty, but is a service of love that is more likely to be accepted by the delinquent. He represents the concerned society, which the offender, deep down inside, longs to be a part of and accepted by, not the dominating society symbolized by police and courts against which his resentment is directed. These lay counselors need not be professionally trained psychologists or caseworkers. They do not diagnose or prescribe, but establish a problem-solving relationship. They should be men and women with better than average education and intelligence, who perhaps have some knowledge of psychology and a lot of understanding of kids; who are respected in their communities; whose experience will lend practical help in the circumstantial aspects of the child's problem; and who will take supervision and in-service training provided by the probation office. Church laymen, teachers, members of the various service clubs, AAUW, and other community organizations can be enlisted by the local welfare associations as volunteer counselors in any community or county.

Furthermore, a parallel procedure can be developed with relation to mental illness. A sizable proportion of the patients now in mental hospitals could be treated successfully at home in their respective communities with the type of volunteer counseling service described above and the fellowship program discussed in chapter 6. Like delinquency, mental illness is basically a failure in love. And, as was stated regarding delinquency, the cure is not solely a matter of accurate diagnosis and scientifically prescribed treatment. These have their place—perhaps an essential place in the more serious cases. However, while medication, shock therapy, and the professional service that only a psychiatrist can give are essential in many cases and helpful in others, it is now being widely recognized even among psychiatrists themselves that the essential cure lies in acceptance, love, the restored capacity to establish interpersonal relationships based on love. The community that has a system of winning these troubled souls into one or another of its little redeeming fellowships and provides a big brother-big sister counseling service motivated by love and supervised by competent professionals can increase the effectiveness of its limited psychiatric service thirtyfold or sixtyfold or a hundredfold.

One of a number of things that deeply impressed the writer while in Europe was the village church at the center of each little community, with a spire pointing skyward. The church was the dominant landmark and once the dominant influence. Two centuries of scientific progress, industrial development, and social change have brought so many services and social functions under the control of secular agencies that the role of the Church and its influence have greatly lessened in modern life. But the ebb of that tidal influence has passed, this observer believes, and the rising tide is coming in. Not that church buildings will henceforth occupy the geographical center of the town or be its most imposing structure, and not that as a social organization the church will take over many new social functions and thus dominate community life; rather, as a human-divine fellowship in which the ferment of divine love is the principal binding and redeeming force, its unequaled worth is slowly being recognized by secular society. Like leaven in the lump of dough, the spirit and influence of the Church, the Spirit of Christ, will permeate all society and its agencies, being felt but unseen in the structural organization of these agencies. But in the field of social welfare where society is confronted with the most intimate needs and deepest hurts of its problem children, the spirit of the Church must not only be felt as a motivating force in the work of other agencies but seen in manifestation, made incarnate through its own agencies and organized program. In alerting the community to its responsibilities, in initiating its own overt action, and in organizing other community resources in co-operative action to help solve the problems of our problem children and neighbors, the churches of the community are finding and accepting a primary responsibility. Like their Master, these churches came into being not to be ministered unto but to minister—to minister through their own and neighborhood agencies to the troubled souls of the delinquent and neurotic, the socially and mentally ill.

NOTES AND ACKNOWLEDGMENTS

Notes and Acknowledgments

Chapter 2

IS YOUR CHILD A POTENTIAL DELINQUENT?

1. Nathaniel D. M. Hirsch, *Dynamic Causes of Juvenile Crime*, p. 30. Cambridge: Sci-Art Publishers, 1937. Used by permission.

2. Sheldon and Eleanor Glueck, *Five Hundred Criminal Cases*, p. 112. New York: Alfred A. Knopf Incorporated, 1930. Used by permission.

3. T. Earl Sullenger, *Social Determinants in Juvenile Delinquency*, p. 19. New York: John Wiley & Sons, Inc., 1936. Used by permission.

4. William Healey, "The Delinquent as an Individual," in *The National Probation Association Yearbook, 1930*, pp. 31-35. New York: The National Probation Association, 1930. Used by permission.
Walter C. Reckless and Mapheus Smith, *Juvenile Delinquency*, ch. 1. New York: McGraw-Hill Book Company, Inc., 1932. Used by permission.

5. Eduard C. Lindeman, "Underlying Social Causes of Crime," in *The National Probation Association Yearbook, 1941*, p. 113. New York: The National Probation Association, 1941. Used by permission.

6. William Sheldon, *Varieties of Delinquent Youth*, pp. 793-800, 829. New York: Harper & Brothers, 1949.

7. Karl Menninger, *Man Against Himself*, pp. 5-8. New York: Harcourt, Brace and Company, 1938.

8. *Ibid.*, p. 203.

9. *Ibid.*, pp. 203-204.

Chapter 3

THE CHURCH IS CONCERNED

1. *A Child Went Forth*, p. 20. Albany: Department of Social Welfare, 1942. Used by permission.

2. *Ibid.*, p. 25. (Italics mine.)

3. George E. Hill, "The Ethical Knowledge of Delinquent and Non-Delinquent Boys," in *Journal of Social Psychology*, Vol. 6, No. 1 (February, 1935), pp. 107-114. Used by permission.

4. Willis D. Mathias, *Ideas of God and Conduct*, p. 101. New York: Columbia University Bureau of Publications, 1943.

5. Pleasant R. Hightower, "Biblical Information in Relation to Character and Conduct," *University of Iowa Studies in Character,* Vol. III, No. 2, p. 33. Iowa City: University of Iowa Press, 1930. Used by permission.

6. Hugh Hartshorn and M. A. May, *Studies in Deceit,* p. 360. New York: The Macmillan Company, 1928.

7. John Edward Todd, *Social Norms and the Behavior of College Students,* Contribution to Education No. 833, p. 100. New York: Columbia University Bureau of Publications, 1941. Used by permission.

8. Sullenger, *Social Determinants in Juvenile Delinquency,* pp. 306-307.

9. Lowell J. Carr, *Organizing to Reduce Delinquency,* pp. 37-38. Ann Arbor: The Michigan Juvenile Delinquency Information Service, 1936.

10. Austin L. Porterfield, *Youth in Trouble,* pp. 109-111. Fort Worth: Leo Potishman Foundation, 1946. Used by permission.

11. Belle Boone Beard, *Juvenile Probation,* pp. 9-10. New York: American Book Company, 1934. Used by permission.

12. *Ibid.,* p. 152.

13. Virgil E. Rowder, "Name Religion as Child Welfare Aid," in *The Christian Century,* Vol. 67, No. 51 (December 20, 1950), p. 1527. Used by permission.

14. Sheldon, *Varieties of Delinquent Youth,* p. 838.

15. *Journal of 1952 General Conference of the Methodist Church* (Lud H. Estes, ed.), p. 1416. Nashville: Methodist Publishing House, 1952. Used by permission.

16. Harold E. Hegstrom, "The Church's Role in the Prevention of Delinquency," *Studies in Spiritual Therapy* in the *1944 Proceedings of the Lutheran Welfare Conference in America,* pp. 44-46. New York: Lutheran Welfare Conference in America, 1944. Used by permission.

17. Leland H. Waters, *The Christian's Attitude Toward Delinquency.* Atlanta: Home Mission Board, Southern Baptist Convention. Used by permission.

18. Elaine Holcomb, *The Role of Religion in the Prevention of Juvenile Delinquency.* (Master's Thesis, Southern Methodist University, Dallas, Texas, 1956.) Used by permission.

Chapter 4

THE PROBLEM CHILD IS RELIGIOUS

1. Holcomb, *The Role of Religion in the Prevention of Juvenile Delinquency.*

Chapter 5

THE CHURCH AND OUR HOMES

1. Elton and Pauline Trueblood, *The Recovery of Family Life,* p. 13. New York: Harper & Brothers, 1953. Used by permission.

2. *Ibid.,* pp. 30-33.

3. *Ibid.,* p. 35.

4. C. Logan Landrum, *Our Delinquent Children,* pp. 4-5. Copyright, 1946, by the Institute of Crime Prevention (Minneapolis). Used by permission.

5. *Ibid.,* pp. 6-7.

6. Ernest Groves, *Christianity and the Family,* p. 105. New York: The Macmillan Company, 1942.

7. Blanche Carrier, *Church Education for Family Life,* pp. 3-4. New York: Harper & Brothers, 1937. Used by permission.

8. John 10:10. (Revised Standard Version.)

9. Proverbs 22:6. (King James Version.)

10. Holcomb, *The Role of Religion in the Prevention of Juvenile Delinquency,* p. 139.
11. Luke 2:52. (King James Version.)
12. Smiley Blanton, *Love or Perish,* pp. 102-104. New York: Simon and Schuster, 1956. Used by permission.
13. Roy A. Burkhart, *I Am the First Community Church,* pp. 4-5. Columbus: Community Books, Inc., 1946. Used by permission.
14. *Ibid.,* pp. 18-20.
15. *Ibid.,* pp. 20-21.

CHAPTER 6

THE REDEEMING FELLOWSHIP

1. Guy L. Roberts, *The Way of Life,* pp. 104-105. New York: Comet Press, 1956. Used by permission.
2. *Ibid.,* p. 107.
3. George A. Warmer, Jr., "A Family-Centered Church," *Marriage and Family Living,* Vol. IX, No. 2 (May, 1947). Used by permission.
4. Burkhart, *I Am the First Community Church,* pp. 9-10.
5. *Ibid.,* pp. 18-19.
6. See Hebrews 11:6.

CHAPTER 7

THE PASTOR AS COUNSELOR

1. From *My Dear Ego* by Fritz Kunkel, pp. 33-34. Copyright, 1947, by The Pilgrim Press, Boston. Used by permission.
2. Carl Rogers, *Client-Centered Therapy,* pp. 171-172. Boston: Houghton Mifflin Company, 1951. Used by permission.
3. See John 2:25.
4. Warren D. Bowman, *Counseling with Couples Before Marriage,* p. 9. Elgin, Illinois: Brethren Publishing House, 1945. Used by permission.
5. See Luke 14:23.

CHAPTER 8

THE CHURCH AND ITS ALLIES

1. John 10:10. (Revised Standard Version.)
2. Emily Hartshorne Mudd, *The Practice of Marriage Counseling,* pp. 263-264. New York: Association Press, 1951. Used by permission of Family Service of Los Angeles Area.
3. *Ibid.,* p. 269. By permission of the author.
4. Richard E. Gosswiller, "Climate of Hope," in *The Kiwanis Magazine,* Vol. 41, No. 4 (April, 1956), pp. 17-20, 55. Used by permission.
5. *Ibid.,* p. 21.